PRAISE FOR
A Glimpse of the Other Americas

"Judi writes in literary style, sharing a deeply personal
journey that is both a look at Central and South America
decades ago and a love letter to her late partner-in-life."

—Fran Golden, award-winning travel writer

"Judi Lifton has written a charming memoir that transports
readers to distant lands in *A Glimpse of the Other Americas:
A Backpacker's Memoir*. I learned about destinations and
cultures I would never have chosen to visit and felt like
I had traveled in her footsteps, whether on a jungle river
in the torrid Guyana rain or a dusty road in Ecuador. Her
vivid writing style lets you feel and experience the journey
without leaving the comfort of your home ... no backpack
required. Two thumbs up for *A Glimpse of the Other Americas*."

—Betty Weibel, author of *The Ohio Literary Trail: A Guide*

"I was born in San Ignacio, Belize. When I read Judi's
chapters on where I was born, raised and lived from 1961-
1998, I felt like I was home again. I know the photos in the
book very well."

—J. Maria Alvarez, Belizean American

A Glimpse of the Other Americas

a backpacker's memoir

Pentagon Gallery Et Cetera Editions

Cover image by Brandon Pierce-Ruhland and Judi Lifton
Passport drawing by Peg Asensio
Cover and interior formatting by The Book Cover Whisperer:
OpenBookDesign.biz

979-8-9860983-9-5 Paperback
979-8-9860983-6-4 eBook

Printed in the United States of America

FIRST EDITION

To Lee ... and our legacy of unconditional love and friendship.

Other Books by
JUDI LIFTON

Letters to the Chief:
A Minnesota Childhood

A Glimpse of the Other Americas

A Backpacker's Memoir

Contents

Introduction

When I was a child and folks asked me what I was going to do when I grew up, I answered, "travel." Everyone chuckled. We lived in a small Scandinavian town called Willmar, Minnesota, and the greatest excitement then was to visit one of the 10,000 lakes. I was an avid reader and took my bicycle down to the library to inhale books about adventure. My older sister said that I was the only person she knew who could read four books a day (in the summer), play with friends, and still get our chores done. By the time my family relocated to Minneapolis in the mid-fifties, my imagination was fueled by exploring the world. *National Geographic* sent me packets of information that were advertised in the back of their magazine. I'm sure that my handwriting betrayed my age but they responded, nevertheless. I filled a humongous drawer with all the information I collected.

After I grew up (so to speak), I had many adventures; I hitchhiked by myself two times through Canada and two times through Europe, staying in youth hostels along the way. I went to Egypt after the Arab-Israeli agreement in 1975 allowed travelers into the country, and flew to Rio de Janeiro for the Mardi Gras Carnival in `77. However, those travel notes are on loose paper in baggies or in mini-spirals, not documented well enough to print. Then Lee came into my life—we took 17 trips, mostly to different countries in Central and South America, intending to save the European and domestic trips until last. All went according to plan for 20 years until Lee got hit by a virulent gastrointestinal stromal tumor

(GIST). Through exercise, diet, and chasing treatments we held it at bay for almost eight years, taking trips (where medical help was available) to Hawaii, Guadeloupe, Puerto Rico and a few southern states in the United States. Lee died at the age of 57.

So, my friends, I'm sharing three of our adventures. I've included photos ... none of them were digitally enhanced, but you get the idea of what we were up to. Our naiveté of world events is evident, but I am glad we witnessed how the Ecuadorians were willing to stand together and face the consequences of a bad regime. I am not certain why I was so determined to share these adventures; maybe to record a glimpse of life, to paint a portrait reflecting a tiny slice of life at that time.

I hope I was successful ...

1983

Belize

~ഉ~

I am part of all that I have met;
Yet all experience is an arch wherethro'
Gleams that untravell'd world whose margin fades
For ever and forever when I move.

—Alfred, Lord Tennyson
Ulysses

CHAPTER ONE

Belize City

The wheels of the airplane hit the tarmac with a thud and we abruptly came to a stop. Our international flight #321 to Belize City was over. Lee unfastened his seat belt and jumped up to get our packs from overhead. "Am I looking forward to two weeks in the tropics away from the ice and snow of Cleveland!" he exclaimed.

I got up and squeezed myself alongside him so I could stand upright. "Happy early birthday present," I replied with a hug.

"Great gift, sweetheart," Lee answered before heading down the aisle towards the exit. Packs on our backs, we walked down the steps and across the asphalt into the terminal. It was warm and sunny and almost noon. Finding a cab, Lee asked the driver to take us to Quan's Lodging. Four weeks ago I'd sent money for our first night in the country and had enclosed a postage-paid envelope asking for a receipt and confirmation. The mailman delivered a sealed but empty envelope. There had not been enough time to make further inquiries. Comforted by the fact that it was still morning and the Belizeans spoke English, the question remained, "Did we have a room?"

"What's the address?" the driver asked.

"21 Queen Street," I replied.

"Oh, I think I know the place. It's in the main part of town."

The airport was a half-hour ride from the city. The road was rough. It slowed us down— gave us a chance to look around and notice it was lush and green. There were lots of simple homes along the road with louvered windows and small front porches pleasantly painted in a rainbow of colors; some very subdued and some very bright. The pastel tones felt calm and quiet; the brightly painted felt happy and gay. A few looked sad and unkempt, their facades peeling or fading.

People of various sizes and shapes were carrying packages from their morning marketing, hurrying home before the rays of the sun would be directly overhead making their loads feel heavy. The potpourris of the locals reflected as many shades and hues as their humble homes.

As the Caribbean came into view, the driver said we were approaching the city. Soon we were riding beside the sea, observing the boats lazily stretched along the water's edge. Across the road, houses stood close together and high up on stilts, looking "on guard" as if fearing for the lives of their bobbing friends.

Our driver kept darting around holes in the road, mumbling about rain and poor drainage. We watched the architectural rhythm change to older buildings in disrepair, seemingly patched and mended by amateur carpenters using any available materials. The cab driver stopped in front of the most inventive facade in view. "Here you are," he said.

Looking out the window of the cab we saw the handyman's nightmare! Two buildings had been connected by second-floor additions. Each annex tentatively "edged" its way onto a common landing. There were crossbeams and steps, but the boxy protrusions gave the illusion of two large bellies juxtaposed.

The posts that supported the second-floor landing extended beyond the roofline and shouldered a beam that held a faded sign which read "Quan's Lodging." The erratically distributed steps somehow finalized it visually (although maybe not structurally).

Just then I noticed a small Asian girl sitting on one of the landings, her legs swinging in space, sucking her thumb and watching us.

Lee looked up at her and yelled, "Is Charlie around?"

A man appeared answering, "You are the two from Cleveland. I have your room waiting."

After paying our driver we followed Charlie to our room. He opened the door and displayed a small room covered in brown paneling with one small louvered window. An oscillating fan on a tilting floor stand leaned over the head of a double bed wedged against the wall. All visible floor space was covered by well-worn linoleum. The paneling, in retaliation to the high humidity and neglect, curled up in despair as it met the flooring; its suspension above the linoleum gave a sense of dilapidation to the room. In harmony with the temperament, a rusting metal chair sat along-side the bed for a token nightstand. The door opposite the chair opened to a hallway leading us to a communal bathroom. In the remaining corner was our "closet"—a piece of broomstick attached crosswise onto pieces of a two-by-four nailed to the wall.

"No one else is staying in this section so you have the bathroom to yourselves tonight. Here is your key. If you need ice, we keep it in our refrigerator and we'll give you a couple of glasses; just knock on door number one."

Lee and I looked at one another and smiled. "Well, we have a room," Lee said throwing his pack on the bed. "Let's get some air and see what Belize City is like."

I placed my pack with his and headed out. Lee locked the door and followed. Placing one hand on each of my shoulders, he massaged them in silent assurance while guiding me down the hall.

We went down the steps to the street; the little girl was still sitting on the same landing sucking her thumb, looking at the world from "her" place. Lee and I could tell she was watching us and we turned and waved. Her available hand lifted in response.

After the hours on the plane, we walked around to stretch our legs and get acquainted with the landmarks. Our spirits were happy and relieved that we had a room. "Let's head for the water," I said. "Sunshine and no responsibility ... can't get better than that." We walked along silently, taking in the sights and smells.

The roads were not paved; there was loose stone. Both of us were glad we had not changed out of our hiking boots, even though they were hot and heavy. The breeze was coming from the sea onto land and we noticed a foul smell in the air—then we noticed the open trenches along the road and the gooey stuff within them. Just at that time, a rat darted across our path. "I thought rats didn't come out in the sun," I said.

Lee laughed, "We've never tested that theory before."

The Caribbean Sea was beautiful! We wandered and watched the fishing boats come in until we discovered a small stand with stools and sat down to eat conch soup with bread. Nearby, there was a boy carving figures out of dark domestic wood and another man working on tortoise shells. It was just the beginning of our journey, so we were not interested in purchasing and carrying any excess baggage. But we sat admiring their expertise for a while before I turned to Lee. "Do you remember the first trip we took together to Merida in 1981?"

He laughed. "Oh yes. I was smitten with you. When we came back from Chichen Itza we stopped at a market before coming back to the hotel. You wanted to take a shower and while you were occupied I ran out and bought you a present."

"You came in the door holding something large wrapped in newspaper. You handed me the package and said it was my engagement ring. I told you I didn't want a ring, so instead, you went out and bought the beautiful expensive jade sculpture of a tiger with a snake wrapped around its body and holding up his jaw that I had seen a few hours earlier. I had loved it but knew we couldn't afford it."

"You were worth it then and still are," Lee said, kissing my hand.

We continued to sit in silence with the sun hovering around us, like a man's best friend, and felt happy just to be.

* * *

WE WERE WALKING BACK to Quan's, rounding the corner to Queen Street when we ran into a couple stopped in the middle of the road having a discussion. The man was laughing. The woman was not! The man called to us and Lee and I went over. It seemed their discussion was over the small high-heeled shoes the woman was wearing. One of the heels had broken off. The man, who introduced himself as Jack, was breaking off the other heel so the woman could maintain her balance while walking.

He introduced the unhappy women with the heel-less shoes. "This is my wife Marilee. We're looking for fishing boats. A friend of mine lives around the docks. We came to Belize to visit him."

The couple really seemed uncomfortable. Marilee looked like she had been kidnapped on her way to a shopping mall wearing apricot polyester pants and a matching leather shoulder bag. Her short blond hair and gold earrings accentuated her eyeleted blouse embroidered with apricot flowers which was sticking to her body. Now, her little white pumps were no longer pumps—she was pissed! Marilee's voice barely remained civil when she asked us a question. "Do you know the direction to the fishing boats?"

Lee and I looked at each other. The couple definitely needed our help! "Yes, we can show you where the boats are. We just came from there," Lee answered.

Off we went. Jack was a talker and very relieved to have a new audience. "I can't believe we're here. Marilee and I have debated for the last few years whether or not to come to visit one of my old friends, Ron. He and I were roommates all the way through Whitman and then law school at the University of Washington Seattle. We even were in the same law firm in San Diego for twenty-five years. Then he split ... craziest damn thing. Used to sail and fish with his wife and family. One day he left a note on the kitchen table and said, 'The boys are grown. I'm fifty. It's time now or it'll never be. Keep everything. I'll talk to the law firm soon. Sorry, Ron.'

"Well, he took his boat and traveled around and finally landed here. Straightened everything out with the firm and gave the profits to his newly estranged wife. They're divorced now. He's contacted me several times and asked us to come down. It's been about four years since I've seen him. He keeps in touch. Says he's selling solar panels, taking tourists out fishing and sailing, and has settled in with a gal named Cindy. I'm anxious to see him. Ron called after he received my letter and said, 'I can hardly wait to see you,' and gave us the name of a hotel to stay in since they just had a small flat."

Marilee spoke up. "We're staying at the Cypress, the nicest hotel in town. It's on the ocean and has a beautiful lobby and veranda on the water, but our room is pretty awful. It smells moldy and is costing $80 a night. I don't know how I'll ever live there for a week. Now my favorite shoes are broken. I wonder if they carry dress shoes here."

Well, I said, "if you look at the way I'm dressed it's obvious that I'm probably not the right one to ask." I paused to see if she would smile or laugh or something and she didn't, so I went on. "I think we passed a few merchants selling shoes on our walk over here." Somehow Marilee just wasn't about to brighten up, at least not now. Her brow was becoming furrowed thinking about the week ahead: living in a smelly room without her favorite white shoes. I was concerned for her welfare. I tried again. "The hotel probably can move you to another room. I wouldn't worry about it."

Marilee started talking. "I didn't want to come, but Jack persuaded me to. He thought being alone with Ron and Cindy might be uncomfortable. Now here I am. We traveled before having our children, Lisa and Ricky. I never wanted to be far away from them. So every year Jack went deep-sea fishing with his buddies off the coast of California. Then I would meet him in Las Vegas, and we would play blackjack and see a few shows. We've done it for years, but Jack wanted to see Ron this year. With the kids both in college, I couldn't get out of it. What about you?"

"We're kinda like you're friend Ron. Both of us have been bureaucrats for over a decade but it didn't suit our ideals or creative spirits. It's good money, but that's not enough. I left last spring and opened an art gallery and frame shop; Lee joined after I got it set up. We love our lifestyle and friends. Income is about one-quarter what it was, but we can still afford to spin the globe once a year and take a vacation. Where did you travel before you had a family?"

"Jack and I took a tour through South America for our honeymoon. It was three weeks and we saw most of the country. Then the next year we had Ricky. I was so relieved that traveling was out of our system."

The two men were walking in front of us. Marilee's shoes kept us out of their conversation and unfortunately, we were doomed to not participate. Luckily, the water was in view. The apartment where Ron lived should be near. After stopping a man on the street, Jack showed him a written address. Jack and Lee started walking again but soon turned into a driveway. By the time Marilee and I caught up, a dog tied to a tree at the neighbor's house was barking, but no one was home at Ron's.

Jack didn't seem upset in the least, "Well, he hasn't changed. We used to remind him of dates with the court and clients. I guess here in Belize no one keeps a calendar for him. Why don't I leave him a note," he said, adding, "Do you want to come back to our room for a drink? I brought some Beefeaters along and I'm sure in this heat we could all use some."

I looked over at Marilee. The furrows in her brow had turned to crevasses: Jack was trying to hold her at bay. We all knew that she had a few things to say to him. Lee and I had nothing pressing to do so we agreed. Changing our direction, we followed the road towards the water and their hotel. A vendor was opening his small store attached to the front of his home. "What is in all those bottles?" Jack asked.

"I brew wine and alcohol. How about trying some?" the man said. "What's your drink?" He took out a glass and awaited Jack's response.

"How about some gin?" said Jack.

The merchant poured him a sample and Jack belted it down.

"Hey, not bad, how much is a bottle?"

"Two dollars."

"Must be great stuff," I whispered to Lee.

Jack paid and took his clear bottle with a screw top from the salesman. "Have anything to wrap this in?" he requested.

We were on our way again, brown-paper-wrapped bottle in hand.

The sun was blazing hot but three of us remained in good spirits. I felt noble saving Jack's day. I could tell Lee did too ... and Jack was thrilled to have our company!

As we approached their hotel, it was obvious that we were in the rich section of town. With the water in view, the buildings were becoming larger and more extravagant. The demands of the tourist faction had been taken into consideration including luxurious hotels. The lavish homes on the beach boasted of the high economic status of rich locals and investors.

Marilee, having a difficult time, was limping and sweating. Her composure was seeping out with the sweat on her body. Turning to me she spoke. Her throat sounded parched, yet, there was a chill in her voice. "How often did you say you spun the globe? Luckily, you found each other, because no one I know would put up with this."

Silence was the only response that seemed appropriate, and

fortunately, we were walking up to their hotel. Maybe I could get Lee to talk to her? I was nearing the end of my patience with Marilee!

The doormen looked magnificent in their crisp white shirts and pants which sharply contrasted their rich, darker skin tones. They greeted us politely as we entered the hotel. I thought one winked at me; I wondered if he had already interacted with Marilee and was trying to tell me to "lighten up, she's impossible."

Jack immediately walked over to the concierge and asked for ice. We all took the elevator and arrived in their air conditioned room. Soon the hotel clerk knocked on the door and Jack received a call from Ron.

I could tell by the tone of Jack's voice that he was fond of his friend. He laughed and chuckled and said, "We'll see you then in a few minutes." Jack told us that Ron had gotten his days mixed up and thought we were meeting tomorrow.

"Lucky he didn't think it was next week," I teased.

We had a drink of the gin from Belize (which tasted very perfumy) and waited for Ron and Cindy before cracking the Beefeaters. Finally, they walked through the door. Ron, alias Santa Claus, wore baggy Bermuda shorts and a white beard. He was accompanied by Cindy; she was the same height but 80 lbs. lighter, wearing cut-offs, a halter top, and a wonderful smile on her leather-tanned face.

I liked her immediately. She walked up and said. "Hi, I'm Cindy," and extended her hand for me to shake. I guess she hoped I was Marilee. I introduced myself. Jack finished the introductions.

Over a cool drink, Jack told how we all met. Santa Claus and Cindy laughed; Marilee had even recovered somewhat thanks to the cool air conditioning.

Lee stood up. "Well, we'd better get going. We have to figure out where to catch the bus tomorrow morning and what town to stop in for the night."

"You mean you haven't planned your trip?" Cindy questioned.

"No, we only have planned to stay away from the coast. We'd like to stay away from the tourist developments and go inland towards the Guatemalan border. Tonight when we go out for dinner we'll ask the locals at the restaurant and the merchants who have their stands along the road where they or their friends go. It's easy for us to do things simply since we do a lot of camping and hiking."

Cindy offered her suggestion. "A neighbor of ours just came back from a very rustic place outside the small town of San Ignacio. It's in the backlands and is run by an English couple who built their house plus three thatched huts on a creek for those who enjoy nature. I guess they're a real 'trip.' Our neighbors thought it was great fun. They're all ham radio buffs and that's how they found out about each other. Want me to see if they would contact them?"

We both said, "Yes." When Cindy called her friends, they agreed to immediately radio Chad and Mindy who "were probably home since minding their simple resort and reading books were their day's activities."

We all regaled one another over our Beefeaters before the phone rang. "Chad and Mindy will be happy to have you," was the response. "Check in at the small store by the bridge and they will radio that you've arrived. It will take about one-half hour for them to come upriver by motorboat to get you."

The first leg of our journey was planned.

We expressed our gratitude and left as "the old law partners" began swapping stories.

I felt sorry that Cindy was stuck. For Marilee to find a sense of adventure and enjoy herself would be a true miracle. My guess ... her entire vacation would be a quest for the perfect white shoes.

I nodded to the doorman as we left the hotel. It was a delight for us to be alone. We could feel a gentle breeze coming off the Caribbean. Our only concern was, "where to eat." It was truly luxurious to be so carefree.

Walking away from the water and into the city, we found a dining place up on a second floor overlooking the street. There was an "improvised balcony" (actually the supporting roof for the marquee of the store below) which meant the customers sat among the wires and support system of the lit-up sign. Thrilled to have a view of the street below, we sat on two available chairs by one of the card tables. Adjusting our chairs we could see either into the dining room through the crudely installed patio doors or down onto the busy street below. The diverse population was noticeable. We immediately felt as though we were part of the melting pot of Belize.

The restaurant we were sitting in was known as Michael's. We learned this as Michael scurried about retelling his story as he lit a Coleman one-burner camping stove on nearby tables to make his stir-fry. We felt the resourcefulness of his spirit, the Belizean pioneer spirit, in his sparse decorations and the illusions he attempted to create with his balcony and make-shift bar that consisted of a group of sofas and an old buffet. Atop the buffet sat a cooler of ice, liquor bottles, and glasses; alongside the buffet stood a man, the bartender, ready for service.

Michael, wearing a white karate uniform and rubber sandals, seemed to enjoy his captive audience. Standing by his primitive stove, using few utensils, and speaking in a soft voice while cooking, he entertained the customers, looking up intermittently to monitor their response to his performance. He seemed oblivious to the rest of the room and didn't notice the man walking up to our table who we assumed was the waiter but in reality, was pursuing another career in Michael's establishment ... drug dealing. His query was direct, "Can I sell you Americans some drugs?" Lee answered, "No," but the hustler continued to pressure us, listing his entire menu and prices.

Offended by his persistence, I stood up and in a loud voice said, "Leave us alone or I will get Michael."

Turning to Lee he said, "Anything for you is half price. You need drugs to deal with a woman like that." Then he disappeared from our sight.

Our waitress appeared and recited our six choices; three kinds of stir-fry, house salad, house soup, or ham sandwich. I realized why Michael was so busy and ordered the soup. Lee ordered a chicken stir fry.

Then we sat and waited for Michael. There were no other cooks. We began adjusting to the rhythm of Belize City. Our metal chairs were not the most comfortable for the wait ahead, but the busy street below consumed our interest. The drug dealer, aka waiter, was busy below stopping people with questions and sometimes going into one pocket or another to retrieve the merchandise that he would then swap for money. Everything he sold was in brown paper. The streets were reasonably well lit, but he showed no indication of concern. I wondered for a moment if his occupation were legal. In answer to my question, I heard a wolf whistle, probably a tip-off signaling that a policeman was nearby, and the dealer disappeared into the night.

The street continued its momentum. Some vendors stood by carts to sell their wares. The shops in the background were beginning to close and their vendors, one by one, turned off the light, pulled down the large overhead door which opened to the street behind them and finally, installed a huge padlock to the closed door. Mesmerized, I felt like I was at the theatre and the huge velvet curtain was closing, leaving a few actors on the shallow stage with the hope of keeping the attention of the audience, not wanting them to go away or drift into disinterest. Fascinated, I watched and waited.

Most of the traffic was leaving. A few people stood talking to the vendors or came up for a purchase. One man sat leaning against a building. His merchandise was displayed on a crate box. He sold Chiclets, cigarettes and matches: individually, in small packs, or the entire pack. How many pieces of gum and cigarettes did this man have to sell to eat, to sleep, to feed anyone else?

Michael disrupted my thoughts as he walked up to our table with his Coleman and wok. "I'll be back in a minute with your food," he said. And he turned about-face and went to get his supplies. Quickly he came back with a plate in one hand containing the stir-fry ingredients and in the other a bottle of oil and tongs.

"I'll bring your soup when I'm through cooking," he said nodding his head towards me.

"Where are you from," he added as he lit the grill, adjusted the flame, and set the wok on the burner.

"Cleveland, Ohio," I responded, curiously wondering how far the conversation would go.

"Home of the Cleveland Indians," he smiled. "I'm a baseball fan although I was raised in England with a cricket field across from my cottage. Since owning this restaurant, unfortunately, I've little time to keep up on sports."

"How did you get to Belize?" Lee asked

Michael put some oil in the wok, looked up, to see if we were interested, and said, "Yes, everyone asks me but I don't mind telling how I came here." And he settled into his storytelling mode.

I focused on him. He did look misplaced. The karate uniform made a statement. His hair was dishwater blond and cropped Dutch-boy style. Under his uniform, he wore a red t-shirt, and from his neck hung a gold chain and gold cross which was very noticeable against the bright shirt. My guess, from observing his profile, was that when soaking wet, his weight was 140 lbs. max, and he was 30-35 (same age as us). Maybe he was a priest that left the Church because he was disappointed with their demands? Michael sounded educated. I stopped my mind from guessing and listened.

"Before I came to Belize, my home was Lancaster, England. I've always been a chef even when I was a teenager. My grandfather had a tavern and employed me just to keep me off the streets. He made money, the old fellow, and taught me to cook as well. Fried a lot of fish and chips 'til I met my girl; her father owned an exclusive restaurant. I met her at university. Both of us became teachers and helped in the restaurant. I cooked on weekends. Pretty soon it seemed we were only saying goodnight to each other. Then one night she said goodbye ... left me cooking at her family business and she left town.

"I was devastated and applied for a foreign teaching position with the English government. I received a three-year appointment in Belize at the country's capital of Belmopan which is inland from here. I didn't know just how much I would miss the water. When my term was up I decided to forego teaching and attempt my own restaurant business. It's been five years and I adore it. If my luck holds out I'll try for 40 more."

Lee's stir-fry was done and so was Michael's story. Somehow I felt the two were related. I was curious about him and now knew a little of his background but I needed a question answered. "Why do you wear a cross on your neck? Are you religious or into witchcraft? It's so conspicuous that I could not help but ask."

"My grandfather not only employed me in his restaurant but insisted that I accompany him to church, that is the Church of England, very regularly. I hated it as a teenager although I realized he was trying the only way he knew. Since I've come to Belize I have become comfortable with a diversity of people and beliefs and now I wear a cross as a talisman. It reminds me of my grandfather and brings me good luck." He paused. "I hope you have a pleasant stay in Belize. Your soup will be here shortly."

The night felt pleasant. Lee enjoyed Michael's cooking and when my soup finally arrived it was tepid but tasty. The drug peddler had returned below. The man with the Chiclets was still sitting by his crate box. It felt tranquil looking down over the street. Conversation became hushed. Michael was no longer in the dining room soliciting comments and the remaining customers were content without him.

Our stomachs were appeased, and glasses empty. Our metabolism had shifted into a mode of relaxation. We probably would have sat there indefinitely if our behinds were used to the folding chairs. Instead, we got up, deciding to walk around before turning in. "Let's try to find out where to get the bus tomorrow," Lee said. "Everyone must know the stop."

We started walking. No one seemed to notice us until the drug peddler yelled from across the street. "My friends come over and say hello. Tell me about America and her wealth." Then he paused and gave a raucous laugh. Some locals turned to stare. We looked straight ahead, embarrassed by the thought of any familiarity with him. As we passed a stand selling beverages the attendant said, "Don't mind him. He's just a noisy man and means no harm.

I apologize for him. Would you like a glass of juice?"

"We just finished eating and are out for a walk, but we do have a question. Tomorrow we're off to San Ignacio. Do you know where the bus stop is?" Lee asked.

Our new friend was eager to be of help and assured us he knew exactly where it was. "It's not very far from here. If you just stay on this street for about five blocks you will cross a floating bridge. You will see lots of boats and fishermen. They make a good living. My brother is a fisherman. Sometimes I help him if my wife runs my stand because it is hard work to sell all his fish before they spoil.

"If you walk by the boats and walk some more you will see a gas station with lots of wrecked cars in a lot next to it. Turn right there and continue down the street. Finally, you will see some buses. You want a blue bus, a light blue bus. It goes to San Ignacio, stopping along the way but you will not have to change. I know the morning one leaves at 7 o'clock because it's the same one I take to see my sister."

"How long does it take?"

"Oh, it depends. The bus leaves when it is full. Weekends it leaves quickly because a lot of people go to see their relatives, but weekdays you could sit there for a while. There is only one other bus and that's at six in the evening. It would be dark when you got to San Ignacio."

We chatted a bit more. Any question we asked he was happy to answer. The info we learned about his country: Most clothing was imported, also a lot of the food. His favorite spot was a tiny island off the coast where he fished and sometimes camped if he was on a holiday. Tourists were discouraged on the island, and only one family lived there permanently. "There's no way for you to get there: You can only visit the islands which have become resorts. I think the people in San Ignacio will be friendly since few tourists stay there," he said. After shaking his hand we started back to our hotel.

Approaching Quan's the street already felt familiar. It was getting dark. The little girl was no longer perched on her landing watching the traffic and the day go by. I wished, nostalgically, for the days when people passed their time by telling stories—when chatting was a way of life. We could have sat on a bench in a park listening and laughing with those around us. But technology and television had begun their invasion. Personal contact and story-telling seemed less important. Families playing and picnicking in the parks were competing with portable televisions.

We knocked on Charlie's door for a glass of ice, had a cold drink, and read until our eyelids drooped for sleep.

CHAPTER TWO

Chaa Creek

Was it the strange street sounds or the stuffy room that woke me up? Feeling disoriented I lay still for a minute before realizing I was in Belize City. The oscillating fan was grinding away, moving side to side in an attempt to push the air. The effort seemed futile. I turned off the fan and checked the clock. It was only 5:30. Hoping the humidity in the air was only reflective of our sleeping quarter, I quietly put on a t-shirt and shorts and walked out onto the landing.

It was barely light and a pink glow appeared on the horizon. To my delight, the air was 15 degrees cooler than inside. Should I wake Lee up or take an hour hike alone? It was going to be a difficult day with the long bus ride ahead. Walking back into the room was like walking into an oven. Lee was already awake and almost ready to go. Within minutes we were strolling out into the cool air, adjusting our packs to fit comfortably on our backs. Following the directions from the evening before, we took a right in front of the hotel. The morning was quiet. People were moving quickly along. Some were talking in soft voices as though "the quiet" were sacred.

Lee and I walked along looking for a place to eat breakfast and watch the local traffic. A merchant was sliding back the overhead door to his restaurant just as we were approaching. Noticing the tables and chairs right on the edge of the sidewalk, Lee asked, "Are you open?"

"Yes," he answered. "Sit down." Shortly, we were drinking coffee with our toast and eggs and feeling the beginning moments of the day, listening to the beat of the feet walking by, and seeing the faces of the people.

After dawdling over our coffee we left to find the bus for San Ignacio, finally discovering a retired school bus painted blue with faded black letters on its side saying "Robert's Bus Line." It was already three-quarters full. As we got on a few passengers looked at us in interest. Most were talking among themselves. I asked a woman about the departure time and she responded, "When it is full." We found a well-worn empty seat next to an open window and put down our packs. "At least we'll get some air," Lee said. "Let's leave our knapsacks to reserve our seats and run over to that stand across the street to buy some juice."

Seven o'clock came and went. The bus had every seat full ... but the definition of "full" really meant packed to the brim with people sitting on the edge of their seats, knees interlocking in the aisle and a mother with two small children sitting on the engine cover at the front of the bus. We finally left at 9 a.m. with the sun as our guide and not a cloud in sight.

The ride was uneventful, hot and dusty. People continuously got on and off. At Belmopan we stopped just when the sun had climbed directly overhead; there was hardly a shadow from the cement government buildings under its rays. My imagination awakened with a jolt: I felt like I had journeyed through an arid stretch of land and all of a sudden stumbled onto a concrete oasis. I looked out the window at the hot cement, its mass giving off mercuric heat waves, and wondered if the town was going to evaporate in front of my eyes. Eventually, the bus drove on, leaving the shimmering concrete behind, unchanged.

It was 2:30 p.m. when we arrived in town. Driving across a bridge and uphill, the bus stopped at a small, quiet square containing a few benches and people waiting for friends. The heat permeated the landscape making every living thing lethargic as though the town were drugged.

Lee and I looked for the "small store by the bridge" where we had been told the owner would radio Chad and Mindy to come and get us. We were curious about their primitive resort and surmised they must be real campers if their property was only accessible via the river.

There was only one store perched right on the edge of the road next to the bridge. Its back end was supported by wooden four-by-four posts adjusting for the steep decline to the water. The owner, anticipating our arrival, had already received a message from Chad ... a few of his cattle had broken their fence but he would come as soon as possible.

"What does 'soon as possible' mean?" Lee asked.

The shopkeeper laughed and said, "Knowing Chad, at least three to four hours. Walk around and enjoy yourselves. He will dock his red boat at the pier behind my store so keep your eyes open. Chad also picks up a few things when he comes to town and won't leave you behind. Don't worry."

Thanking our messenger we walked out into the warm air to explore the drowsy village of San Ignacio. Many of the stores were closed for a siesta, but we continued to wander hoping to find a place to stop for a bite to eat. Our breakfast seemed long ago and our snack was just a cookie and a shared carton of juice. Lee and I walked up and down the streets of town smiling and saying "hello" to the residents. It seemed like a friendly enough place. Most of the people were gathered around an open field. As we approached, we could see there was a traveling amusement park setting up rides.

The carnival workers were very entertaining as they took the sections off the truck and magically built the rides for tomorrow. The children were spellbound. Not far from the activity and close to the river we noticed a building, up on stilts, with a large over-hanging roof and open windows. It was an ideal place to look for our captain, yet stay entertained with the carnival in full view.

Walking up the steps we came into a bar full of men. They were not eating but were sitting by the tables drinking and playing checkers. Everyone looked up when they saw me; I ignored their stares as Lee and I sat at a table. "There are no other women here," I whispered. Just then a waiter walked up. He appeared somewhat nervous and turning to Lee he asked, "Can I get you anything?" He never took his gaze from Lee's face.

"Do you have anything to eat?" Lee asked.

"Only chips," the waiter said.

"I'll have two beers and three bags of chips," Lee replied. "We've just come in from Belize City and are waiting for a friend. This is the only place open we've seen."

"Kim's will be open in two hours. They have the best food in town," the waiter said, again directly to Lee before walking away.

Our beer and chips were delivered. Our backs to the audience, we stared out the window across the open field pretending to be mesmerized by the assembly of the amusement park rides. No one came up and requested that we leave, and neither of us asked if my presence were appropriate. The only clue was from a small child who ran up to retrieve his father from one of the checker games and said, "What's that lady doing here?"

* * *

IT WAS A WONDERFUL place to sit. A slight breeze whispered ripples down the river: The water disappeared into the lush foliage. On the bank within our view were a few women washing clothes under the shade of an enormous tree. The overhanging limbs also protected their children who were splashing and playing nearby. The air wafting through our window was calm, warm and comforting. Our traveling spirits felt at peace with our decision to visit the Belizean countryside. "A beautiful spot isn't it?" said Lee.

"Yes, it is," I replied and silently reflected on how grateful I was to be with him. We had worked together at Corning Glass in the late '70s. I was a department head and he was a ceramic engineer. It was the days of recruiting women for management and I was the only female among 1500 men. I loved the industrial environment and must admit it was empowering. I had a policy not to date anyone employed by the company; I even wore my hair in a bun to appear more serious. Lee was interested in dating, but I said that I couldn't because of gossip and visibility. He replied, "I was thinking of looking for another job, anyway (which later he told me was fictitious)." Ruby, one of the office helpers would tease any time she saw me, "I can tell he has his eyes on you," and then she would laugh. Meanwhile, Lee actually did change companies. He was sought after, top of his class and experienced. Well, the rest is history, and here I was sitting looking at the Macal River in Belize and very happy that Lee had persevered.

* * *

CHAD'S BOAT WAS STILL not at the pier but we did not dare stay any longer. Another beer without food in our stomachs would put us to sleep. Getting up, we said goodbye to our silent companions and left the establishment. One man responded audibly. A few nodded. We walked down the steps and across the field. Now, feeling slightly revived, it seemed appropriate to walk around. Maybe we would find "Kim's." If Chad was late we would leave a message at the store and go to dinner.

Up and down the streets we walked, checking out the scenery. A few of the storefronts had come to life but we weren't eager to buy anything, especially at this point in our travels. There were three or four bars, all similar in appearance, with overhangs to the street and an Old West-style wooden swinging door showing a dimly lit space within. A few men were standing outside with bottles enjoying the warm afternoon. The rest, if any, were inside telling stories and continuing the ceremony of generations ... the hunters and breadwinners swapping new and old folklore with a drink in hand and a story on their lips, competing with one another for details of a well-worn tale.

We continued to walk, saying hello, nodding to adults and children who held hands and giggled. Some were so shy they looked down at their toes in discomfort.

The houses were lined up high above the ground on stilts, giving the family an outdoor area under the house that was protected from the rains. Hammocks swung from the rafters and clothes hung haphazardly from lines. Smoke from small fires and boiling pots meandered around objects and finding any open space drifted into the sky and disappeared.

There was no wind, but it was cooling off a little. Inspecting the side streets we did not discover "Kim's" restaurant but instead found two bakeries and a small grocery store. As we came up over the hill we arrived back at the small square that the bus had left us at a few hours before. Buying a banana from a vendor, we sat on a bench watching people. Their movements were picking up. The heat had abated. We bought another banana and decided to walk down to the pier to wait for Chad.

Sitting on planks that connected the pier to the land, we dropped our feet into the water as we continued to wait. The river was quiet. The women were no longer washing clothes. Turning our backs to the town, we looked downriver at the dark green forest. A bird flew silently by. It felt like nothing existed but us and the river.

Moments passed ... then I thought I heard something ... the sound of a motor. Soon a boat and man came around the bend. "It must be Chad," I said.

The man and his boat composed an interesting picture against the backdrop of the jungle and the water. He was dressed all in white and was blond and fair. The boat beneath and around him was lipstick red. He sat as motionless as a wax statue. The boat moved toward the dock. "Look," I whispered to Lee, "He could be a British actor on-site for 'Out of Africa'; even his rolled-up sleeves look starched."

Coming within hearing distance he said, "Hello, my name's Chad. I assume you are the two who will be coming to stay with us. Sorry, I'm late, but there were troubles at home that I needed to tend to. I would like to pick up a few supplies before we're off. Mindy will keep dinner until we get home. Maybe you would like to get a piece of fruit or snack to hold yourselves over while I shop? I'll tie the boat up and we'll meet back here at half-past five, all right?" And he disappeared up the bank.

We pulled our feet from the river. The warm air instantly dried them. I could now understand how people swam in the river without taking off their clothes ... it would be only minutes before they were dry. Putting on our shoes, we walked up the bank to the road. Neither of us wanted any more fruit but we remembered the bakeries we had seen earlier that day and a sweet and coffee would tide us over until the agreed time. Knapsacks on our backs, we retraced our steps.

There is something very delicious about having coffee and cookies and looking out open doors onto a street observing the local traffic at its natural best. The bakery clerk's child, supporting our philosophy, kept watching us. Our little friend finally got up the nerve to come over as we were ready to leave. "My name's Natty. What's yours? Are you going to live here forever or are you with the carnival?" she asked.

This was a tempting moment for me. Never having an opportunity to work in a carnival, this may be as close as I got! Lee must have read my mind and quickly gave the young girl our names and admitted we were visiting Chad and Mindy "down the river." I could tell Natty was disappointed and I figured that we could still save face so I said. "Well, I once had an Aunt Ida in a circus, does that help?"

"Really," said Natty, "What did she do?"

"She was a snake charmer. Aunt Ida would play a very pretty tune and a big snake would rise from his sleep, stretch way into the air and move his head around. She could make him do magic!"

Natty stood and smiled. "Did the snake have a name?"

Lee interrupted. He started putting on his knapsack (maybe because I was a good storyteller and he knew we might miss our ride) and turned to Natty. "I'm afraid we have to go," he said. I finished my storytelling by dubbing the snake Pickles. Natty laughed at the name. Saying goodbye we headed for the pier.

Lee asked if I really had an Aunt Ida in the carnival.

"Yes, she was a disgrace to my father's family. I'm not sure if they ever got over it. They still talk about it even though Ida ran away when she was very young. One of her close cousins, Aunt Jenny, used to get postcards from her. But even Jenny wouldn't believe that the cards were from 'real' experiences. *How could she possibly be having such a good time?"* she would say.

* * *

WE CAME DOWN THE river bank right behind Chad. He untied his red boat and we jumped in. His clothes still looked impeccable. It seemed unbelievable that he had chosen this place and at this time ... even if his parents had abandoned him and fled back to their homeland, this was not the turn of the century where he would be forced to remain in exile; I watched him as we followed the river. Chad didn't say much, just opened up the motor and moved along; somehow the noise seemed too loud for the environment. Here we were in the Garden of Eden; the foliage and wildlife was surrounding us, and our captain was zipping down the river. The bank rose high above us. I felt very small. It would not have surprised me to see the face of a tiger, the decorated body of a man with a protruding spear in hand, or even to hear the voice of some spirit saying, "This is my land and you are blessed to be part of it."

We saw no one. The greenery was overwhelming. An occasional unobtrusive house sat high upon the bank. The only noise was the small red boat bringing the three of us up the river. All of a sudden the boat slowed down. Chad said, "There are some rocks here but I know them well. After the next bend, you can see my home."

But the river gods must have moved the rocks, or Chad wasn't concentrating because the boat met the rocks with a calamitous sound. The motor became silent. "Damn!" Chad said. After pulling the motor up and checking things out, he added, "The shear pin broke. It takes forever to get parts! Give me the oars so I can get us home."

The bend came up much more slowly now that he was rowing. I did like the peacefulness and the sound of the oars dipping into the water. I doubted Chad agreed with my thinking. He actually showed rings of perspiration on his starched white shirt by the time we came near his house.

Someone saw us coming and came running down the bank to meet us ... a little blond girl and a small Mayan woman. "Who's that?" I asked.

"My daughter Ginger and a housekeeper," he answered. The mystery of Chad's presence in Belize was an enigma. It would be interesting to find out his story.

Ginger greeted her father warmly. "Daddy, what happened to the motor, the boat is so quiet?"

There was kind of a grunt and then he responded, "It broke. Now you and Helena show these people to their place, OK?"

We followed them up the hill. It was very steep, but the path curved to accommodate the incline and steps had been created by digging out some earth and bracing the remaining dirt with boards. I spoke to Ginger. "Can you walk up and down these steps in the rain?"

She laughed. "Mostly we go off and see grandma in New Orleans when the rains come. But I'm not allowed on the steps anytime it rains. One time I came up from the river with my Daddy when it was raining. He was carrying some packages. I couldn't hold his hand and had to walk all by myself. I slipped and fell and got real scared."

We climbed to the top and were standing on a plateau. To the left, on a knoll, were two small square structures joined by a veranda. To the right were three thatched huts. There were small valleys cut in the face of the hillside and I could see walkways bridging the solid sections of land. There was another hill in the distance with cows contained by a barbed-wire fence that wandered around the huts creating a maze.

"Can the cows put their noses in our hut?" Lee asked.

Ginger giggled. "No, but they can stretch pretty far. Your hut is the last one over. Come on. I'll show you."

As we walked single file behind Ginger towards our hut, Helena, smiling and speechless, brought up the rear of our short line. The little girl enjoyed the experience of the three adults following her and would run ahead, turn around and wait for us.

"Here we are," she said opening a gate. We entered a tiny hut propped on a hillside built in the same style as centuries before. There was a bed and a long crude bench with a candle and matches sitting on it. The only signs of the 20th century were the sheets and pillowcases. The hut had a palm-thatched cone-shaped roof.

I looked up to see a structural framework of beams and poles extending to the ground all made from bark-less tree limbs which were notched and held together with vines. The high roof had a significant overhang before support poles went into the ground and were joined in a circular four-foot-high wall of naked tree trunks. The lower wall became a stockade with a gate for the door. The top half of the wall was nonexistent. There were no screens or windows, no interior walls of any kind, and no mosquito nets over our bed.

Helena started to lead Ginger away. "Aren't there any mosquitoes here?" I asked.

"It's windy. There aren't any bugs here."

Helena uttered some words in Spanish.

Ginger turned and pointing her small fingers, said. "The toilet is over there and the shower is up there. My mom will ring a bell soon for supper." They walked off. Looking to the right was a mini-hut like our own identified by Ginger as an outhouse. If we would be sitting or standing our occupancy would be visible. Lee and I looked at one another and laughed. "I know several people that would definitely be constipated staying here," I said. And we laughed again.

Up the hill a ways was the shower, the same design but built with higher walls. Lee was 6'2" and his head would show above the stockade. At 5'2" my head wouldn't show, but if there were other residents, since there was no door, I would probably wear a swimsuit rather than be naked. There was a steel drum sitting on a flat platform overhead holding air-temperature water, and all we had to do was open the one spigot and start washing. The imagery of ourselves, or anyone we knew, standing in the shower kept us laughing and talking. "We have to take a picture," Lee said.

Just then we noticed a huge moth resting on one of the posts.

The camouflage was superb. The wings, straw-colored and relaxed, opened away from its body. The span must have been at least eight inches. It was breathtaking to see and made me feel I was truly in an exotic foreign land.

We heard the clanging sound of a bell. "I think I'll find our flashlight in case we're talking into the late hours. Maybe we'll find out how this place came to be," I said.

Lee thought I was funny. "Maybe it's their deep dark secret and they won't answer your questions."

We started walking over and Ginger came to guide us. "I'm hungry. Hurry up."

She jabbered away as we walked to the house. Ginger was six and next year would be attending school in San Ignacio (where we had been picked up). She had a new brother by the name of Kyle who she did not like because he cried all the time. Both Kyle and Ginger had been born in the very house where we were going to eat dinner. By the time she had told us this information we had arrived at the veranda and Chad was ushering us into the kitchen to eat.

I could see Helena out in the backyard as we walked up to the house. Another small Mayan woman served us fried plantains and leathery pork chops. We were starved from our bad eating habits that day and ate everything without comment.

Mindy was in the adjoining room bedroom attending to the baby, which left the four of us eating together. Ginger led the conversation. (Chad seemed distracted.) Her main topic seemed to be school and the fact that she would have to stay with her aunt in town because she could not go back and forth every day. I asked her if she would mind staying in town and Chad interrupted with the fact that he went to boarding school when he was six, so Ginger was very lucky that she could come home on weekends. "Besides, we go to town often and will check up on her."

Mindy came out of the bedroom to introduce herself and to retrieve Ginger for bed. We left the table and moved out onto the breezeway which connected the structure we were in with another. The design of the building was one long roof built over a cement pad. The area under the roof was divided into three equal sections. The first section (closest to the river) was a unit that contained the kitchen and bedroom. The next or middle section had no front or back wall but rattan padded furniture which was facing out towards our hut. The last section contained an office and sitting room. Large doorways from both structures faced the middle section or breezeway. There was a dim light on in the office allowing us to see the interior. The furniture was more comfortable in that room than where we sat, but our view was absolutely breathtaking. It was dusk and the light was quickly fading. Lee and I sat there speechless as we absorbed our surreal surroundings.

Looking to the left I could see the cows wandering and hear their bells telling us of their presence. To the right, the land sloped to reveal the dark glimmering surface of the river. Straight ahead was our small hut with its thatched roof pleasantly awaiting our return. I was about to comment when I noticed Chad sitting silently rocking. His hands held a large snifter of brandy that he swirled as he rocked, looking at the liquid as though he were seeing his melancholic reflection.

I said nothing but was relieved when Lee interrupted Chad's thoughts saying, "How do you keep your food from spoiling? All I saw in the kitchen was a large stove."

"The refrigerator is standing against the house over there," said Chad, and he turned around in his rocker and pointed. "It uses propane. The rest of the house we run off a generator that uses gasoline." Saying no more, Chad leaned back and continued rocking.

We all sat in silence watching the darkness move in ... like a dimmer switch slowly turning. Momentarily, Mindy came out; she had just put the two children to bed and seemed ready for conversation. As she sat down I asked her about the dried garland and long ribbons hanging on the gable of the office and living area. "Oh, that's from our wedding," she said.

"Did you meet here in San Ignacio?" I asked.

"No," she said laughing. "One summer I went to London with a girlfriend of mine from New Orleans. We had just finished our junior year at Tulane University and had talked our parents into giving us a few weeks abroad. We saw Chad at the famous 'Lion and Lamb' pub. From my dreams, I remembered a man who looked just like him. Night after night I dreamt of the two of us sailing on a boat. Well, there he was, and I knew it was meant to be. Chad had just settled a family feud and was scheduled to leave for Belize in one week. It was love at first sight and he asked me to be his pioneer bride."

I looked over at Chad. Yes, he had a mystique about him, but I think she had more than her hands full. He sat looking down into his snifter, frozen; the only thing that moved was his eyelids.

Mindy smiled. "His father was putting heavy pressure on him to settle into the family business. Chad was 24 at the time and his father felt he had played around enough. The family business was jewelry, and while Chad had an older brother who was a craftsman, his father thought Chad could be a financial wizard and wanted him to take the business seriously. My father-in-law never saw eye to eye with Chad. Maybe it was because for years he had sent Chad away to private schools and they never got to know one another. Chad didn't want to join the business. Then his father blew up and told him that if he were going to be a playboy he'd have to support himself. Fortunately, his aunt came to the rescue.

"Aunt Rose was visiting from Belize and said that her husband, Edward, had won some land in one of his gambling adventures. He was in the military and was stationed here. Uncle Edward died from a heat stroke two years before we moved here. Rose offered Chad the land if he would pay the back taxes. She said it would make a wonderful resort if he set his mind to it. My father-in-law gave Chad the money saying good riddance and that never again would he have the option of the family business. I came into the picture right when Chad was about to leave. No one approved of our quick romance. I went to New Orleans and got my things. We met in Belize City and immediately got married. It's been seven years. I can hardly believe it. Aunt Rose and I are great friends. My mother comes over quite often and loves it here. Chad's family has never come. They took his leaving very hard, I guess."

Chad interrupted. "I have my own empire here. Next week I am going to Belmopan to try and get permission to cut a road through my neighbor's land. At one time he agreed to give us access. Without it, we can't make a good resort out of this place. Now we have to park the truck one-half mile away and walk in."

Mindy had a sense of humor. "Maybe if you wouldn't have run over his dog when you came in drunk one night, things would be different." She laughed.

"Maybe you can work something out," Lee said. "Buy him another dog or something."

Chad turned and somberly addressed Lee. "At this rate, my only recourse may be to kiss his feet and buy him a dog!"

Seemed like a good time to leave for our hut. I looked over at Lee; he looked ready too. "Well, we enjoyed our dinner. We'll see you in the morning."

"Breakfast is at seven-thirty," Mindy said.

Saying our goodnights we found our way to our hut. The stillness of the night embraced us. It was time for all creatures to sleep. As we lay down, my drowsy mind was contemplating the whereabouts of our huge dozing moth.

* * *

I HEARD BELLS, SOFT and inconsistent like those high in the mountains of Switzerland. They were calling me to listen. Was I dreaming? It felt real. I opened my eyes and saw the thatching above. Then I realized I was in Belize sleeping in a hut on the banks of the Macal River. I didn't feel like moving. The soft music and the cool breeze of the morning felt harmonious to my being and I wanted to lay there endlessly drifting in my thoughts, feeling the euphoria of being in this place. Today would be slow and easy, without any travel on dusty hot roads. We could relax and explore our cool, lush environment.

I was smiling to myself at the pleasure of it all when a young voice kept yelling, "Judi, Lee, where are you? Mommy has breakfast ready and waiting." And while bursting through the gate of our hut she added, "Hurry up. I'll wait. Breakfast will get cold." Then Ginger proceeded to sit on the bench by our bed and continue talking. "Get up and let's go."

Pulling the sheet up to my chin I responded. "Why don't you go and then we'll get dressed?"

"That's ok, I'll wait," she said.

"No, you won't nosey. Now beat it."

Ginger ran off laughing and saying, "You remind me of my Aunt Rose. She calls me Snoopy."

Lee mumbled, "Here we are in the middle of nowhere and

some little kid is running our lives. Unbelievable."

Walking over to the house, we passed a group of cows by the fence. Their dark eyes looked like wet glassy marbles. Their bodies appeared transfixed, with tails and mouths operating independently, swishing and masticating in robotic motions. Their movements were unchanged upon our passing.

Breakfast was waiting and so was Ginger. Mindy was feeding Kyle his cereal. Chad was nowhere to be seen. Ginger sat about two seconds before starting to chat. "We're going to town with Daddy to bring the broken motor. Why don't you come along?"

Mindy aborted the suggestion immediately by saying, "I've asked Helena to pack you some sandwiches and a jar of juice. We'll be home in time for dinner. A friend of ours, Mick, is coming with his sister from Cancun. He wants Chad to give her a tour of Mountain Ridge Falls. You may go along if you wish. The cost is $15 a person. Let us know at dinner."

We drank our thick murky coffee and ate our marmalade on bread as Ginger proceeded to tell us, "I was helping Daddy take the motor off the boat this morning and we saw this fat long snake. I was scared but Daddy said it was a 'safe' snake. I have to tell my Aunt Rose when we go to town, 'cause she knows all about animals. This snake was so big I think he could have eaten my whole arm in one swallow."

Helena smiled and placed some fried plantains on the table. Lee loved the banana-squash-like taste. I thought they were chewy and dry.

Chad appeared and told his family that he was ready to leave, inquired how our sleep was and left before we had a chance to respond.

Mindy said nothing of his rudeness but mentioned there was

lots of coffee. In response to Chad's command, she picked up the diaper bag and handed it to Ginger, then taking the baby out of his chair, she gave Helena his bib and followed Chad. We watched as they all disappeared into a field that they had to cross to get to their truck. I was beginning to understand why their neighbor had not allowed them to cut a road through his land and felt that maybe he was generous to permit them to walk through his property.

Excusing ourselves, Lee and I took our coffee and went onto the veranda to absorb the coolness and the quiet of the morning. The house sat on a knoll higher than the rest of the property; we looked over the land feeling like the residing land barons reflecting on our magnificent estate. There was so much green around that the landscape exuded life: the trees were inhaling and exhaling, their breath cool upon our faces. Green parrots were flying around fostering illusions as we sat, Lee in Chad's large wicker rocker and me in a matching chair, feet up on the rattan coffee table. Sometimes Lee rocked or one of us muttered a few words, but mostly we sat on our pedestals looking over the land letting our thoughts wander.

Helena brought us a fresh cup of coffee and disappeared without a word. We continued to sit, the tranquility invading our bodies and minds. Finally, feeling energized and ready to explore, I went into the kitchen to find the juice and sandwiches and mistakenly knocked a pan off the dish drain into the sink. I startled Lee into reality! Then we left our knoll to explore the new world we had chosen.

As we were walking towards our hut we could hear laughing. It was distant and unclear. Where could it be coming from? We stopped to listen. There were woods to the front and rear of us and the grazing cows on the left. We heard it again and both started walking towards the river. Our view of the water was from high on the bank looking down 100 ft. Precariously positioning ourselves, we lay on our stomachs and looked over the edge to see Helena and two other women swimming and laughing, their heads bobbing above the water. For a few moments we watched, removed from the action but mesmerized by the dark figures swimming below us against the backdrop of the green velvet bank.

It felt tempting to join them but then we weren't invited. I whispered to Lee. "I wonder if the snake Ginger told us about was real."

"I don't believe I would like to find out," he responded.

Just then I noticed something moving in the grass. It was a parade of large ants each carrying a bit of leaf and moving rapidly in a line. Showing Lee, I said, "Look at all those ants madly going somewhere." Then slowly I took one of my white socks off and left it in their path. They walked over it, rather than around it. The backdrop of my white sock made the stream of ants look enlarged and unreal; like watching a parade of monster bugs in a science fiction movie. It brought back a childhood memory of when I attended a marionette show. The lights were low and all eyes were focused on the stage. In the end, the heroine was dragged off by a beast. The audience was stunned and quiet. Then the lights went on and the hands and heads of the marionetteers were displayed alongside the stage. The audience gasped and screamed in cathartic relief. Somehow the story seemed relevant as we watched the bugs march up and over my sock ... an element of distortion bound them together.

Finally, I used a series of sticks to detour the parade around my sock. We got up to follow the ants, to see where the infinite stream was going. But their route proved too complicated.

Deserting our bugs, we went back to our hut.

It was peaceful having no one else around and especially con-
venient when needing to use the outhouse. Never in my life have I
sat atop a hole in a wooden box surrounded by a short chest-high
stockade fence and a small roof perched on two poles overhead,
smiling out at the cows and a jungle river. I have dug a hole in the
ground or used a traditional outhouse but never sat upon such a
grand throne to do nature's business.

I was interrupted by Lee yelling and pointing. I looked and
saw two strange exotic birds in the tree ten feet from where I was
sitting. Were I not in such a compromising position, I would've
sworn upon seeing the bright gorgeous birds perched on a branch
that I was dreaming about a mystical garden instead of living it.

Soon we were walking away from our hut into the interior
along a path carrying our juice and sandwiches, the two birds flying around us. Our destination was unknown, but with the visible
markings of traffic, we were unafraid. The forest was peaceful; its
quiet interrupted by occasional bird songs and the sound of our
feet. It made me wonder how the pioneers chose their site to settle.
Did they behave similarly to us and follow the most well-trodden
path and then at some point stop and say, "Voila, we are here?"
Or did they camp out and physically explore the terrain and its
outer horizons and then finally choose? We continued walking
along, turning our heads up and around, while the sun smiled
down through the greenery overhead giving us encouragement
and warmth.

Who knows how long we walked? It was timeless and addictive.
As we came to the end of the trail there was a clearing with a large
hut in the process of being built. The frame was tied together by
vines and the thatching of the roof had just begun. We looked
around the clearing for the path, but it had stopped. Then we

realized the structure must relate to Chad and Mindy. Sitting on a pile of felled branches with leaves, we ate our sandwiches and discussed how the new hut related to our hosts. All possibilities for construction were explored. Our favorite one: A private aviary for the raising of birds accompanied by an eccentric ornithologist who lived with them. After creating our description of fictitious Hugo and his exotic birds and stretching our imaginations to particularize all the details, we continued our walk.

Deciding to stick with our exploration of the neighboring property, we veered from our path but headed obliquely in the direction of the house. This should put us on the hill where the cows were grazing, yet, if we became confused, we would have a view of the river and could always find our way back. The going was not that easy. We each picked up a stick to swat the grass alerting all snakes of our presence. Progress was slow, but as long as we kept walking up an incline we were headed in the right direction. When we arrived in the pasture, the grazing cows did not mind our invasion of their turf. They continued to chew and walk. Any change in their direction was indicated by the sound of their bells. Finally, we found a huge tree that we could sit under and survey the property from another angle. It was high on a hill peering down at the world and far into the distance. We felt ecstatic to find this vantage point! Drinking our juice, we whiled away our time watching the birds and feeling the tropical air.

We heard a noise in the distance and two people appeared riding towards the house on a motorcycle. "That must be Mick and his sister," Lee said. "There's no one to greet them."

Soon they parked their bike and went onto the patio, disappeared, came out with a drink in hand and sat in the chairs that Lee and I had used earlier that morning. "I guess they know their way around," I said.

We sat and watched for Mindy and Chad to return. It didn't seem appropriate for us to make our appearance. Ginger and Mindy finally came running out of the field acknowledging they had seen them. Ginger was yelling and jumping. Mick swooped her up in his arms and swung her around, a smile on his face. Then he kissed Mindy and kept swinging Ginger around. His sister hadn't moved from her chair. Chad came out of the field carrying Kyle and yelling at Mindy to come and get the baby. Lee and I continued to sit, hoping that they would all go inside and allow us to remain invisible. Finally, they disappeared from view. We raced down the hill to clean up before dinner.

It was a new experience to wash my hair in a shower designed for our primitive hillside lifestyle. A metal drum contained river water that had been pumped up the hill. The 50-gallon drum sat on stilts seven feet high over a small stockade. A pipe from the drum was attached to the inside of one of the walls. When I turned a spigot, the showerhead sent cold water onto my body. Lee and I took pictures of one another, soapy heads and grinning faces showing above the wall and bare feet protruding below. We looked ludicrous!

Within minutes after getting dressed, Ginger was running towards our hut yelling in her now familiar voice. "Dinner's ready and you can meet Uncle Mick and his sister Emily."

"I didn't know he was your uncle," I said upon her charging into our hut.

"He's not my real uncle." She laughed. "He's my pretend-uncle, 'cause he comes out and visits a lot. He makes Mommy and me laugh. Then sometimes he and my Daddy play checkers and they yell at each other. It's very fun."

We followed Ginger across the hills. "Let's leave if we don't feel comfortable," Lee said.

"I agree."

As we approached, laughter was in the air. We were given drinks and seats on the patio. Introductions were made. Mindy's face was aglow. She was talking to Mick. Chad was looking out over the hillside while casually listening to Emily. I sat silently gazing into the distance relaxing after a good day.

Helena came and announced dinner was ready. We all adjourned to the kitchen for our evening meal. I was placed between Mindy and Chad and across from Mick. Lee ended up sitting by Ginger and Emily. No doubt who the lucky one was! Oh well, I didn't feel that conversational anyway. I would just sit and observe.

* * *

THE EVENING STARTED PEACEFULLY. The weather and setting were perfect. But the warm winds shifted when Mindy asked us a question. "Where did you go today?"

"We hiked and saw a hut being built. Is it yours?" Lee asked.

Chad responded. "It's a friend of Mindy's, an old college roomie that's now a shrink and wants to write a book. She has a theory about isolation and creativity and wants to live alone in her hut for a few years. After Liz graduated from Tulane, she moved to Chicago, received her Ph.D. and has been analyzing ever since. When I met Mindy in England, Lizzy was traveling with her and continuously giving advice about my father.

Mindy laughed. "Chad doesn't like her because she told him to be more tolerant of his father."

Chad responded, "She told me to 'suck up' to him and it was none of her business! I must have been crazy to let Mindy talk me into Lizzy coming to live here."

Mindy laughed, "I begged and pleaded for months before you finally gave in. You'll adjust. I can't believe that Lizzy will last that long anyway. She's only come down to visit a few times and never stayed longer than two weeks. Now she's taking a sabbatical to write a book. It should be interesting. Besides, it would be nice to have a female friend around here for a change. You have Tim to talk to, remember?"

"Who's Tim?" asked Mick. "Do I know him?"

"He's a taxi driver in San Ignacio that I drink with," said Chad. "An English chap born and bred in the same social class as I."

"Was he rich, too?" asked Emily. She seemed so well-mannered that her question surprised me.

Mindy answered, "Tim's father is rich but that is all we know. He joined the military and ended up in San Ignacio. After his term he stayed, married a local girl and drives a cab. Chad and Tim regularly cry on each other's shoulders, especially now that they found a place that carries ale. It's a real-life drama of the prince turns pauper, right honey?"

At this point, Ginger interrupted, "Don't you remember, Uncle Mick? One day after shopping, Mommy and I found Daddy having beers with Mr. Tim. Mommy was mad 'cause Daddy was acting silly. She tried to find us another way home."

"That's right. That was the day the two of you came up to me in the square and asked if my motorcycle was for hire. I didn't realize Tim was the guy Chad was drinking with." Mick started laughing.

Mindy glanced over and smiled.

"Time for bed, Ginger," Chad said turning to Mindy with fire in his eyes. Obviously, this conversation scratched a festering wound.

We were barely midway through the meal and I was already feeling asphyxiated sitting between Mindy and Chad. He was always jiggling his leg and she acted tense, making me feel very "wedged," like the peanut butter in a sandwich. It wasn't appropriate to leave since no one was done eating. Their tension absorbed my appetite. It was a relief when Mindy got up.

Ginger, oblivious to the dissonance, proceeded to hug Mick and Chad and went into her bedroom.

Mick, trying to warm the chill in the air, turned and directed his question to Lee. "Are you and Judi coming with us tomorrow? It would be fun to have you along. Emily wants to see the Hidden Valley Falls, and since you've traveled all this way you should definitely come. I've seen them twice before and they are spectacular!"

"Count us in! Do we leave early in the morning or what?" Lee asked.

By now Chad's blood pressure seemed to have stabilized. After taking a sip of wine he responded, "We leave after breakfast and are gone most of the day."

A day! I, for one, did not enjoy being around this man. His social skills were nonexistent and his sullen behavior was totally unattractive.

Emily chimed in, "You two must come! It will be fun! Besides, these two guys are too serious for me to handle alone. I'm so looking forward to this. Mick has talked about it so much."

Mindy appeared for a minute and got Ginger some animal crackers and milk. She passed the box around. We each grabbed a few as Emily reminisced, sharing how she and her friends in their preschool years used to sit at her kitchen table and tell stories about the animals in the cracker pile and laugh and then eat them until there was not a cracker crumb to be found.

As she talked, I thought the image she elicited would make a good advertisement for the crackers. "What animals are safe and small and make all children in the universe feel happy?" And then there would be a picture of selected children of the world seated in a circle dressed in their native dress with a glass or container of milk appropriate to their culture and animal crackers in their hands, sharing the moment, faces aglow, adorned with smiles and milk-mustaches.

I didn't vocalize the picture to the rest of the group since the conversation had already shifted gears. Mick was talking about his job as a guard on the Belize-Guatemalan border.

"How far is the border from San Ignacio?" asked Lee.

"It's about 20 miles but I don't recommend traveling there right now since there have been quite a few incidents of guerrilla agitation. It might be dangerous for the two of you. Why don't you check out the Xunantunich Mayan Ruins which are about five miles from San Ignacio and save Guatemala for another time?" he advised.

"Do buses go there?" I asked.

"You can always take a cab or there are cars that travel up and down the road and collect people who are waiting on the roadside. That's a lot cheaper."

"How do we know who they are?" Lee asked.

"You 'just know,' and there's nothing to worry about," Mick said.

Mindy came back and joined us after tucking Ginger into bed. She suggested that we go onto the veranda and have a drink. Lee looked at me and shrugged, signaling it didn't matter to him. I spoke up, "We've been outside since this morning. The air is spectacular and the country beautiful but I think we are whooped. You guys enjoy yourselves. We'll see you tomorrow."

"What time is breakfast?" Lee asked.

"Eightish. I'll send Ginger over," Mindy said. "I'll pack a good lunch for you since you'll be gone most of the day. You can bring your suits in case you decide to swim in any of the pools."

Saying goodnight, we found our way in the falling darkness over to our hut.

It felt like we were living a fairy tale with the sky as our windows and the wildlife as our friends. Our mascot moth was waiting for us, attached to its spot and resting for the night. We crawled into bed, propping ourselves up to look out into the night. We felt the darkness move in just like the tide of the sea, silently and quickly. The moon was absent but stars flooded the sky, twinkling, reminding us they were the same stars today as yesterday and the same stars over our native home ... and they would be the stars of tomorrow.

* * *

IT SEEMED BUT A FEW moments before the stars had vanished and light appeared. It was morning. I lay thinking when I heard this young voice calling "Judi, Lee, time to get up; time to go with Daddy and Uncle Mick to the Hidden Falls."

The fearless young leader had found us.

"Here we go again," Lee muttered.

Ginger, breathless, ran into our hut. "Come on and eat your breakfast. Emily and Uncle Mick are already eating. They want to get going."

"Okay, Ginger, but disappear. We'll be there in a few minutes. Adios amigos," I said.

She laughed and ran out yelling, "Hurry up!"

Shortly we were sitting by the table eating our toast and marmalade, repeating yesterday's menu. Lee ate his plantain and mine too. I stuck with the toast. Emily and Mick were chatting. Our friend Chad was his normal blissful self. Mindy, Ginger and Kyle were missing. "Where's Ginger?" I asked.

"Here I am," she said as she came running out of her bedroom. "Mommy and I were talking about what to do today. Maybe I'll help Helena wash clothes or help Mommy sew me and Kyle shorts."

Mick seemed very amused. "I didn't know you were a seamstress, Mindy."

Emily interrupted. "When are we going? I'm anxious to see the sights you've been talking about. Can we all fit in the front seat of the pickup?"

"I'll have you rotate," Chad said. "Judi and Lee will ride with me and the two of you can ride in the back. You'll switch coming down."

"Do you have a thermos so we can bring some of this coffee?" I asked. "It's really great stuff."

"It's Guatemalan," Mindy replied. "Mick walks over to Guatemala and buys a few pounds before he comes to see us. Otherwise,

I occasionally buy it in San Ignacio but it's double the price. There's none left from this morning to send with you. Besides, in a few hours, you won't want anything hot."

After finishing our coffee we went to get our suits and towels. Somehow the prospect of swimming and splashing didn't appeal to me at the moment, but then maybe it would be so warm and dusty riding in the truck that a swim would be wonderful!

As the four of us walked towards the truck, Ginger shouted in the background, "Be sure to catch a frog for me. I need one. My last one ran away."

Mick yelled back to her, "We'll try. See you later."

After walking through a large field, we arrived at the pickup. "Do you think that your neighbor will ever let you cut a road?" Lee asked.

"At the end of the week, I have an appointment in Belmopan to ask the zoning board for a variance. I'll get it eventually. I just haven't found the right people yet."

Lee and I climbed into the front seat. Being the smallest I sat in the middle. I was relieved to see a tape player and hoped Chad would use it. Awkward silence didn't sound like the ideal way to drive up the mountain. To my delight, within minutes Chad was playing a tape of the Eagles and cranking the volume way up, enabling Mick and Emily to hear the music through the open windows. The rear window was immovable so any conversation between us was impossible, but at least we could see if they were still with us.

Mick and Emily looked uncomfortable sitting together on a crude bench with a straight back that was wired to the wheel well and the cab of the truck. I was hoping they had a cushion between their butts and the bench. Noticing another bench opposite them in the truck- bed, I figured Chad or Mindy either drove their staff to town, or they had more visitors than we thought.

The road was winding and empty. Chad knew the sharp turns quite well and took them "one-handed" as he fooled with the tape player and simultaneously pushed down the accelerator. The speedometer needle wasn't moving (which seemed strange since the truck was reasonably new). "So," I asked Chad, "what's wrong with your speedometer?"

"Nothing. I don't have one since Tim needed it for his cab. The police rarely bother anyone, but being a Brit, the odds are against him if they decide to give out tickets. He supposedly is ordering me one but I doubt I'll ever see it."

After seeing that ray of compassion within Chad, I smiled to myself. Maybe despite previous indications, there was hope for him after all!

Even though he appeared to be driving as reasonably as possible, the drive still seemed long. The scenery was rich and green but I loved the feel of the river and the openness of their land by our hut better. We didn't see any wildlife, although I'm sure there was plenty. Any creature would have to be deaf in order not to be frightened by the sounds of a truck crunching on gravel accompanied by loud music.

After bouncing along for maybe an hour we stopped to take a break and have a glass of juice. Emily lit a cigarette. Noticing their cushionless seats, I asked how their backsides felt. Mick laughed. "Wait until you take the ride down."

Lee said, "Why don't you sit on all the beach towels and swimsuits."

The two siblings agreed that Lee was brilliant.

The next hour of riding was uneventful. I still hadn't seen any animal dead or alive. Finally, rounding a curve Chad spoke, "Look at the falls. They are beautiful." And indeed they were.

We stopped at a lookout a little farther down the road. A short simple wall of stone protected the viewer from falling over. Steps allowed the more adventurous to walk 40 to 50 feet down into the valley and rest at a dirt landing where there was a pile of stones discouraging any further descent. An additional deterrent was the white memorial cross leaning to the right which had been wedged between the rocks. Along the precarious sections of roadside these crude white crosses were common; a flimsy marker for the life that was.

Chad stayed by the truck and conversed with a man he seemed to know sitting in a car by the lookout. The four of us walked down a path to a lower landing to take pictures and view the falls. The mist from the falling water joined with rays of the sun and gave us a beautiful rainbow. The transparency of the colors made a shimmering veil over the falls giving the impression that this was an archway into some ethereal place. We stood awestruck. The scenery was breathtaking. Finally, we started walking back to the truck. Chad seemed to be immersed in conversation with the same man. His chattiness amused me. He had uttered only a few words to each of us. Mick commented as we were approaching. "I see them passing a cigarette back and forth, maybe he's smoking some weed and will give us a toke! This trip would be wild if our senses were out of whack. Don't you agree, Em?" asked Mick.

"I don't know. I like the ride without anything extra and it surely doesn't make me feel comfortable having some smoker at the wheel," she replied.

Chad was laughing hysterically. Wow! I thought. This guy is laughing. In three days I hadn't even seen him smile, why the change? Then he confirmed Mick's theory.

Acting very chummy Chad spoke, "Come on, ready to go? My friend here just sold me this good stuff. Do you want any?"

Lee and I both declined.

We climbed into the back and the others jumped in front. "What did we get ourselves into?" I asked. "Maybe we should hitch back to their place. There aren't too many roads to choose from, and people do speak English, so we should be able to make it back. What do you think?"

Just then Chad started the truck and lurched forward.

"Damn!" I said.

The music was blaring as we held onto our seats for dear life. We did not go back the same way but went down the other side of the mountain. I swear he threw the truck into neutral and just followed the winding road as it turned and turned like the coils of a spring. I hammered on the window and Mick turned around and waved. I hammered again but Chad didn't even turn his head. The two men were smoking and laughing. Emily sat in the middle seat. Why wasn't she yelling? She had vocalized disproval.

We flew by another white cross. I hoped Chad had not been the reason for its construction. It was difficult to think positive when we were hurtling down a mountainside with some type of laughing maniac at the wheel, foot off the brake and spinning around the corners. "I'm getting out and walking home if this sucker ever stops," I yelled to Lee.

"I agree!"

It seemed like an eternity before we stopped. Every moving moment my emotions had two faces, one of elation from knowing we were still on the road and one of anger directed at Chad for taking our lives so casually.

When we stopped, I started yelling at him. "What the hell do you think you're doing? If you want to kill yourself that's fine with me, but I enjoy life. You are so selfish that I can't believe it. We're walking home and telling everyone we see what a major jerk you are!"

Emily looked upset. Mick and Chad started laughing.

"Can you draw us a map so we can hitch?" asked Lee.

The men continued to laugh. Just then I heard a car coming down the road. "Good," I said. "Here's a possible solution to this dilemma."

Lee and I turned to look, hoping that the approaching vehicle would take us back to the river. Emily and the guys were talking in low voices. I could tell she was trying to reason with them. Mick and Chad continued to think everything was "funny." We watched a truck approaching. Maybe our problem was solved.

I could see two adults in the front seat. They slowed down; three kids were wedged between baskets of plantain filling all available space in the back bed. The driver hung his head out the window.

"Engine problems?" he asked.

Emily was the one that responded. "My brother and his friend have had too much to drink. I'm taking over the wheel, but thanks for asking."

"Are you going to let her drive, Chad?" I asked.

"Yes," he replied.

"You folks alright, then?" the truck driver asked.

We nodded and he took off down the road.

Chad turned to Lee and said, "I don't trust women drivers. Would you drive? I'd feel better."

"What a sexist," Emily interrupted. "Just so you don't drive."

As Emily and I climbed in the back I questioned Lee, "Do you mind driving?"

"I couldn't do any worse than that joker," he said closing the tailgate.

Emily and I sat on the same bench. Smiling, she turned to me and asked, "Well, on a scale from one to ten how do you rate your vacation in Belize?"

I hesitated before answering her. There were many things to consider. Belize was beautiful and the reception from the locals fit the quality of the landscape. Chad needed to be disregarded in my consideration. After all, I thought, we could at this very moment be riding in the back of someone else's pickup or be yelling and fighting with Chad. Emily had rescued us. A favorable response was in order.

"Well," I said very seriously, "If I minimize the presence of Chad by calling him a foreigner, and maximize the grandeur of the terrain and friendly Belizeans, then I guess I would have to say our vacation rates a nine-and-a-half."

She burst into laughter. "I think you get a grade of ten for your political ability. But I have to admit that this is rather an unusual experience for me also. Since Mick moved here two years ago to become a border guard, he has been begging me to come. I'm glad I came. Upon my arrival, he immediately insisted on my meeting Chad and staying in his home. Now, I realize that Mick's real interest is Mindy. I think he wanted me to come just to divert any possible suspicions about his friendship with her."

"It seems rather risky to be interested in her. The rage that would be expressed if Chad discovered any concrete evidence … his actions appear so reckless that I hope Mindy watches out for herself. Maybe you should warn them to be even more discrete. Tell Mick that we both noticed their intimate looks," I said.

Just then, we went around a bend in the road. Lee swerved and we almost fell off our seats. As a question was forming in my mind I saw the answer lying on the road. A large rock had rolled down the hillside.

Emily interrupted my thoughts. "I'm glad I called Chad's bluff or it would have been a disaster. I think I've pumped my share of adrenaline for a while! I surely hope that they packed us a decent lunch. I'll think about my brother and his dilemma, but Mick is old enough to get in any situation he wants to."

We kept moving down the mountain. It was quiet and peaceful. On occasion, I noticed a well-trodden path wandering up the hill or a simple house standing against the hillside. As the truck hurried down the road, three people were walking from our view. A woman was holding a basket on her head with one hand; with her other, she held the hand of a small girl in braids. A young boy walked behind, his face watching his toes. Along each side, he gripped a heavy bag by handles. The bag was so full and big, that with each step the bottom almost hit the ground as he walked, reminding me of an ox with yoking, destined to do his task forever.

We were silent for the remainder of the descent. I couldn't hear any music coming from the front, but looking through the window I could see Chad and Mick were talking about something. Lee wasn't involved. The two talking seemed light-hearted enough, and I only hoped the substance they were smoking wouldn't start any true confessions or precipitate any angry bouts. We still had some sightseeing that was promised and a lunch to eat.

Finally, we arrived at our next stop. Lee turned off the dirt road and parked on stone along the river. Across from us, some trees grew up a steep bank. Our side was flat and quite rocky. The river followed to the west along the bank, and to the east flowed from an opening in the hillside. I assumed this was the mouth of the cave we would be exploring.

Chad was ready to show us one of the "wonders of his world." He pointed over to the entrance. "I'll show you the cave." Following his lead, we walked on the larger rocks to cross a shallow part of the river. Since all of us had on walking shoes (except Chad who wore hard-soled loafers), we enjoyed jumping from rock to rock and successfully made it to the landing at the mouth of the cavern. On Chad's last leap he was not as lucky; his leather sole slid down the side of the rock. Miraculously he somehow did not fall, but landed on both feet in the water. Profusely swearing as he joined us, Chad emptied his shoes saying, "I love these loafers. I gave money to this American guy from Denver to buy them. I always wear these loafers and never fall in when I bring guests here; I don't understand what happened."

No one commented. No one dared. Emily walked away and asked anyone listening, "Are those dripping rocks stalagmites or stalactites? I never really paid attention in my geology class."

I could not help myself from responding immediately. "Ahah, you brought up a weakness of mine: mnemonic devices. I wasn't into geology either but I know stalactites because the word has the letter c in it for ceiling, making stalagmites the deposits on the floor. After all these years, I can't believe I still remember that."

Emily and I both laughed. Mick looked over at Lee. Shrugging he said, "You get used to it after a while. Sometimes she invents such a difficult system to remember things that I would find it easier to retain the original information."

"But that's how I remember," I responded.

Chad walked over still grumbling. "Here's the cave," he said. "Why don't you look around or take a swim? You'll find me outside when you are finished. I'll be sitting in the sun drying my shoes so they don't stretch. The cave doesn't go any deeper than you can see from here. If you want to go swimming, there's a small pool next to the highest elevation. The water comes into the cave from the mountain and it's quite deep there. After you are through, we'll have our lunch." And he walked away.

"Hey, just look at the bright side. What if we'd come all the way from Belize City for this fine tour," I said.

All of us were in pretty good spirits. Somehow the whole thing was such a disaster that it was funny. Mick piped up saying, "I can understand why he wore loafers. He thought he could walk on water." We all laughed and groaned, our echoes repeating in the cave.

The large stone chamber, amplifying our voices, announced our arrival to any living creature within hearing range. Suddenly there was a splash in the water. All of us heard it. Mick was wound up, "Do you think a bat fell off his perch and died from our laughing?"

"I know my brother's jokes are pretty bad, so let's get out of here before he starts singing," responded Emily. We followed her advice and began to leave. Mick followed her cue as well and brought up the rear of our small group singing, the echoes following behind.

Chad was waiting, basking in the sun. His shoes rested by his side. "Done so soon? What is all the noise about?"

"Oh, you just missed one of my brother's comedy routines," Emily answered. "Why don't we eat our lunch?"

Chad opened a brown bag and gave us each a sandwich wrapped in wax paper. There was a large thermos of lemonade and some cookies, not much of a *repas* for our strenuous day. We sat and looked at the water. It was quite peaceful. Mick remembered that he had promised to look for a frog for Ginger. Chad mentioned that we had one more stop at a series of pools further down the road and that we could more likely find some there.

Soon we were off. Emily and I kept our seats in the back of the truck. She chatted away while smoking a cigarette. "I'm so glad you are here. It would have been an unexciting time without you. We're going back to San Ignacio tomorrow and then to Belize City the following day. Would you join us in either place for dinner? We could share a few laughs about today together. Maybe you could help me work on Mick so he doesn't tangle with these characters."

I realized that she didn't seem that eager to spend time with her brother. The same biological parents don't necessarily make all siblings best of friends. "I think we're leaving tomorrow, too, but we're headed towards Guatemala. There are some ruins we want to see here in Belize and maybe we can find a room in a small border town downriver from there. On the map, it doesn't look very far. Since Mick works around there I'll have to ask him if he knows a place we could stay."

"I know he lives in San Ignacio and works on the border so it can't be too far," Emily replied.

The truck was slowing down. I guessed we were at the pools that Chad was talking about. It was a pretty place with porous soft-edged rock and puddles of water resting here and there. It was not rainy season and some of the standing water appeared stagnant. I imagined there must be a river nearby that came roaring around the corner when heavy rain fell.

Chad got out of the truck. I think he was sobering up now. His words and smiles were disappearing. "Let me show you where the water comes down from the Hidden Valley Falls that we looked at earlier today. The water splits. The majority of it used to go into the caves but now it comes this way," he said. As we rounded a bend we saw the beautiful falls of Mountain Pine Ridge pounding down in front of us. Mist hung in the air as the water moved along.

"If you keep walking you'll see a place where you can walk behind the falls. I'll stay here and wait. My shoes have just begun to dry."

That guy is a real sportsman, I thought to myself. We were having a good time despite him, but Lee got the worst of it having to drive around on strange roads.

I was last in arriving at the falls. The other three were waiting ready to walk across the ledge behind the falling water. The ledge was about four feet wide with a curtain of water falling in front of it. When the falls hit the water and rock 20 to 25 feet below, a sound was created like a far-away thunder that echoed against the stone wall behind us. As we cautiously moved across on the wet rock, the rising mist came through the veil of water. Lee was behind me. I stopped and said, "This is like a scene from 'Raiders of the Lost Ark,' only they walked across a 20-foot tree suspended over a canyon with the bad guys chasing them."

"Just keep moving," Lee said. "You can tell me later."

Emily and Mick greeted us on the other side. "Totally eerie," said Emily. "I watched my feet very carefully. It did not feel inviting to fall to the rock below."

"I still think it's like a scene out of 'Raiders of the Lost Ark,'" I repeated. Mick disagreed and thought it was exactly like a scene from a John Wayne movie where he and two women were riding horses.

"I only remember him in open spaces and hiding behind rocks," I replied. "Plus I never remember him riding with two women."

Emily thought I was funny and Mick attempted to persuade us that we all had just enacted one of John Wayne's scenes.

We then walked down a path back to the pools. All of us were relentlessly quizzing Mick and he was enjoying every minute of it! He was a good sport and countered all our inane comments graciously. Stopping by one of the more stagnant pools he said, "Let's all look for a frog for Ginger. I promised her that I would at least look."

Wandering off, the four of us kept our lookout for a frog but there wasn't much activity. I walked over to the clear water and looked to see if there was anything visible. There were some minnows swimming and a few dragonflies on a rock near me.

All of a sudden Lee yelled, "There's a couple over here. Get a container."

"I'll get one," I responded and ran over to the truck to see what was available. Chad was sitting in the front seat, head back and sleeping. I noticed the thermos on the floor and ran back to the trio with my find.

It was amusing to see the three adults splashing around and seriously trying to corner the frogs. All eyes were glued to the rocks. "We've got to keep them from getting back into the water or we'll never catch them then," Lee said.

Finally, after one escaped and the other almost followed, Lee caught one and asked for the container.

"Here," I said presenting the thermos.

Mick was elated with my choice. "Hey, let's give it to Chad and tell him he can have the last drink of lemonade."

We made so much noise that Chad woke up. Mick welched on his idea and gave the thermos to Emily and said, "Hang on to it."

Lee got behind the wheel and we started for home. Chad put a tape in on "loud." Emily and I took our seats.

"I'm so hungry that I could eat a horse," Emily said. "I hope we can have a snack when we get in. Maybe we could get Ginger to trade us something for this thermos."

"We'd better crack the lid and wedge it by the spare tire to keep it upright or we won't have anything to trade," I replied.

It was a more enjoyable ride going home. The sun was warm but not blistering. I was contemplating how bizarre life was: Coming to a new country, feeling in awe at the green bush and jungle and then finding two people similar to ourselves planted by circumstance in the same place. Maybe Emily was thinking the same thing, I don't know. She was leaning her head back, eyes closed, tanning her skin. I could feel my face beginning to burn. It was already densely freckled and while I did love warm climates, my Scandinavian ancestry predisposed my fair skin to be genetically unprepared for the bright rays overhead. I was debating with myself about putting on a hat versus the value of leaving it off and feeling the sun and getting burned when Emily spoke.

"This ended up an enjoyable day. Being silly with my brother makes me feel like we're kids again. We used to be inseparable until he got into sports. Today made me nostalgic for those times."

It seemed Emily wanted to say more and didn't, but then maybe I read between the lines. I guess I just didn't feel like questioning her. We were slowing down almost to a stop. I noticed three white crosses and thought maybe they were meaningful. However, we continued to move slowly and after a group of trees, we came upon a remarkable sight! There was a complete interruption in the momentum of the scenery; no trees, no rocks, just a collection of hills. There were small, medium and large hills on one side of the road rolling towards the horizon as far as we could see. They seemed strange and naked ... only dressed in the long grass. What happened to the trees and other trimmings?

The truck came to a halt and we all climbed out. "Look at that,"

Lee exclaimed. "Chad told us that this was used for the British army to practice their maneuvers. It must have taken them forever to clear the land. I wonder if they seeded it with prairie grass. Watch how it moves in the wind and picks up the light. It's beautiful!"

The grass moved in time with the wind; a huge bed of glowing golden threads undulating in the sun up and down the hillsides. In the valleys, the shadows made the grass look like rippling water, moving and gray against the backdrop of the sunlit hillside. As the grass faded into the horizon, the sky and the grass blended: there was no distinction between the two. The sun was just at the right place and as the light hit the grass in the distance, the hills faded into the sky just like the water does to a skyline at magical times of the day.

"How long has it been since they used this?" I asked.

Chad had climbed out of the truck to join us. "It's not but a few years. There's still a base in San Ignacio but they're withdrawing more troops every year. We want our independence so they are giving it to us."

We all stood watching the dancing grass. Lee came over and put his hand on my shoulder. "Just think how spectacular it would be to put a cabin on the highest hill and view the world."

"I'd want a porch wrapped around the entire cabin. Wouldn't that be great?" I said.

Both of us smiled. Since 1980 when we started living together, we had hiked, camped and explored our state of Ohio to find a good site for a cabin. We had recently found a plot on a precipice overlooking Lake Erie and had just built a 10 x 15-foot screen house with 4-foot walls where we hung a tent from posts that supported the roof and cooked over the open fire. Our dream was to buy the surrounding property and build a cabin. We had both been raised in small towns and loved the water. Lee was raised on a river and I grew up around one of Minnesota's 10,000 lakes. Building the screen house was an adventure. We used a chain saw to cut the boards and clumsily figured out the structure. It made us stronger, this talking and planning; treating each other as partners in our decision making. My reverie was broken when Lee dropped his arm from my shoulder and said, "Time to move on."

All of us got back into the truck. Mick offered to sit with his sister, but I told him I was alright. As we drove away the clouds were moving in (the white fluffy ones). I wished we could watch to see how they would meet up with the golden fields. Maybe the clouds would look like they were dancing.

* * *

Down the road we went, the grassy hills left in our dust. Emily and I were both pretty mellow by now. Bouncing around in the back of an open truck bed does that to a person. I no longer needed to think about a hat since the clouds had caught up with the sun, so I looked at the sky and all around me. Not many people were out; I suppose the shopping had been done earlier. As we continued down the road, the frequency of white crosses decreased and the road improved.

Emily and I watched the terrain level off and the land become more open and treeless. Soon we were driving down the dead-end road by Chad's place.

Lee relinquished the keys to Chad and we all walked across the field toward the house. Emily wondered, "When are we going to eat? That lunch was a bit sparse for my liking."

"We'll be eating right away after we all wash up," Chad replied.

Ginger had seen us and came racing, "Did you find me a frog Uncle Mick, did you?"

He proudly handed her the thermos with a Kleenex stuffed in the opening. "He's in there?" she started giggling.

"Hey, we drink out of that. How can we use that for drinking?" Chad asked. "Wash it out."

"That's all I could find," I said.

Then Mick piped up with his bad jokes again: "Maybe you'll find a toadstool in there."

"Mick, do you have to?" Emily inquired, and then we all broke out laughing. It was too much even for Chad ... he smiled for a second.

Mindy was okay about using the thermos. She helped Ginger get the frog out. "I see you all had a good day. There are some gin and tonics or beer if you want any. Dinner will be soon."

We were back in moments freshened up and drink in hand. "How did you like the falls?" Mindy asked.

"They were beautiful," Emily replied. "It was the best sight of the day. I'm glad that Mick invited me, and I might even come back. Of course, Judi and Lee won't be here. I tried to talk them into having dinner with us in San Ignacio since we're all leaving tomorrow, but I guess they have other plans."

I was watching the two women as they talked. Emily seemed confident. Her voice was clear and she used eye contact when she spoke. Mindy seemed rather frazzled. Her bangs were long and her eyes were partially covered. When she talked it was as though she were talking to herself. Neither she nor Chad seemed the sort to choose isolation in a primitive environment. Their choice seemed so austere! But who am I to choose the personality profile of a pioneer?

Mindy turned to me. "I didn't know that you were leaving tomorrow, Judi. We'll have to get Tim to pick you up in his cab since Chad won't be available. He's going to Belmopan to check on getting a road cut to our property. Maybe they can force our neighbor to cooperate."

"Can't you buy an easement from them?" Mick asked.

"He won't even talk to us," Mindy responded.

The topic was discussed at dinner. Chad seemed to feel he could make it happen. I wondered what else we didn't know about the situation that was making it so difficult. The four of them seemed eager to talk. Lee and I dismissed ourselves after the meal was finished. We wanted to sit by our hut and look at the stars. Hugging Emily and her brother, we exchanged addresses and said goodbye knowing they were leaving early in the morning.

It was a beautiful night. Entering our hut we were greeted by our large sleeping moth hanging on the thatching as in previous evenings. We quietly moved the bench that was next to our bed outside. Sitting with our backs against the hut wall, we gazed up at the stars.

Looking out into the night the atmosphere was tranquil. The trees across the river stood stalwart and calm. The dark green flatland to the right separated us from the main house on its high plateau. The ceiling lights of the veranda illuminated four people, their gestures clear, but their words soundless—like actors "signing" for the deaf.

The cows, sentinels of the cool grass, kept vigil; their bells soft and comforting while crickets created our background music courting one another in alternate notes, the volume changing at the whim of the participants ... their serenade becoming a lullaby to our ears.

Nature's other musicians remained silent. Every bird and breeze lay quiet and still.

CHAPTER THREE

Benque

I felt the breath of tropical air upon waking. I opened my eyes. Our moth was gone; off to do her daily insect catching or whatever moths do all day. The cows were nearby, their bells interrupting the silence. No human voices could be heard: only the chirping birds singing a cheerful Belizean song reminding us to get up and begin our day. I lay wishing for one of our feathered friends to chirp a personal "farewell," realizing that our hut on the river bank would not be our home after that morning. But my wish did not come true. Instead, our little hostess Ginger came running across the grass telling us to come over and get breakfast and that Tim, the cab driver, would be there soon.

At breakfast, Mindy presented us with a handwritten bill. It did not read "daily room charges plus tour plus drinks." Instead, it was meticulously broken into infinitesimal parts. Each day there was a charge for having the radio on "in case" we received any calls (unlikely, since no one knew where we were). Then there were the two actual calls: one from Belize City and one for the cab ride of that day. Of course, we knew any alcohol we would be charged for ... but for a thermos of coffee we did not, nor did we know that each day we would be charged for Helena sweeping our hut. Then there was the initial boat ride down the river which we thought was for "the ride." Wrong! It was for each rider.

I was so outraged that I was speechless ... my confrontational spirit lay dormant. In retrospect, I can only surmise that from sleeping in the fresh air, with thatched rafters overhead, the breezes must have carried my wits away.

So, in silence, we paid the invoice, in full. Then, picking up our knapsacks, we started across the field as we heard Ginger yelling, "Goodbye," from somewhere in the distance.

"I can't believe they so nonchalantly asked for all that money. I assumed they would be like us in small business: they would be fair and honorable," Lee muttered.

Beyond the field, I could see Tim waiting by his cab. Not good timing in my mind. I was still smoldering and needing some "space."

I greeted him with, "How far is it to town? I'm kind of in a bad mood and need some fresh air."

"It's a long walk," Tim answered. "I drove out here, might as well take you. Get in."

While Tim was driving down the road to San Ignacio, Lee asked him about transportation to the little towns nearby.

"There are special cars that ride up and down the roads picking up and dropping off people that are within the distance they are allowed to drive. The license plates are different so you can distinguish the cars. It's a very inexpensive ride and the only way to get around. There are no cabs or buses that travel those roads. Don't worry, you'll figure it out. By the way, where am I taking you?"

"Just to the top of the hill by San Ignacio," Lee replied. "We're just thinking about how to spend our day. How far is the Guatemalan border from here?"

"About 30 minutes. If you are going today you should leave

right away since the drivers only run in the mornings. I should tell you there's no lodging at the border, just in a small town a few miles away called Benque."

As we drove up to the small square Tim pointed at two cars. "Those two travel up and down the road you're speaking of. Go stand there when you want to leave. He'll wait until he has a full car leaving. He makes more money that way."

After dropping us off, Lee and I sat on a bench moaning about our expensive stay ... I looked up at Lee. "That place was so gorgeous it's unbelievable, but they shouldn't get away with charging like that. It was 50% more than we thought. Maybe we should write the Belize Tourist Bureau. What would we have done if that were the last stop on the trip and we didn't have any more money?" I asked.

"I don't feel like talking about it," Lee said. "Let's move on to Benque and see if we can find any lodging. Looks like that gray car is ready to leave."

The driver was happy to see us. His car was now full. As we rode along he proudly showed us the sights, focusing all of his attention on us. The woman next to me felt she needed to say something and loudly announced, "He talks so much I think he is getting old."

No one else interrupted as he continued on, pointing to the Mopan River and the ferry that could take us across to the ruins. He even knew the hours. "He will take you across and back from 10-3 every day."

Considering us his only audience, he would quickly drop off or pick up passengers. They didn't seem to mind being ignored. Maybe they were relieved? The driver would clear his throat, signaling that he was resuming his chat. It was quite amusing listening to him. He was proud to have relatives in Houston that he would visit someday. After asking us where we lived, and Lee responding "Ohio," we realized that his geography was pretty rusty when he asked for our address so he could stop and see us on the way to Houston.

Soon we were in a busier place. We had arrived in Benque.

"There are two lodgings in town. I'll drop you at Oki's. There is another place further down the road, but Oki's is the best."

In a few minutes, he stopped. "Ask anyone where to find me. My name is Carlos," he said as we closed the car door.

We walked up a few wooden steps into an open storefront. A man came out from the back and stood behind the counter. "I sell cola and tapes of famous singers. What would you like?"

"Do you have rooms to rent, too?" asked Lee

"Yes, many rooms. There are ten rooms here. All are empty but I will show you the best one. There is one with a private toilet that is very nice. Follow me," and he flashed a smile. I noticed a few teeth were missing but it still was a very nice smile. We followed him out the front door and around to a stairwell outside of the building. I realized that he was very short because I was looking directly at the back of his head as he was using one of the many keys on a huge ring attached to a long cable which would automatically retract into the shiny metal case clipped to the waist of his pants.

He turned around and smiled. "There are many locks on these doors so there will be no troubles. I work very hard to have a nice hotel." Again, he pulled the retractable key ring back towards the door and unlocked yet another lock.

Opening the door to the second floor, we turned and walked up an interior enclosed stairwell. The steep steps were dimly lit by the light that drifted up the stairs. I looked around for a hanging lightbulb but didn't see one. I debated whether I dared ask if he furnished flashlights with the rooms and decided against it. Oki stood on the top landing pulling on his fine keyring. There were still two more locks to open. I was beginning to wonder about this man and what if there was a fire. I had never considered fires in hotels until now and wondered if the subject should be brought to his attention. I ventured a question as he was unlocking our door. "Do you turn all those locks at night?"

"Yes, at 11 o'clock everything is locked."

"What if there were an emergency, like a fire?"

"Then you stomp and yell very loud and I will let you out. Don't worry, this is a good building and very safe. I lock the building to keep the drunk-rowdy people out." He opened the door and showed us our room. The bed consisted of a metal frame with coil springs, a wavy mattress with white sheets and two white flat pillows and a blue blanket folded on the end. There was a closet that contained a sink and toilet and wastebasket. No cabinet, mirror, table, chair or lamp was present. One window was over the headboard almost at ceiling level. It was similar to a basement window.

I quickly asked, "Can we open the window if it gets stuffy?"

"Yes, it is a nice window; I just put it in. Do you like the room? It is five dollars and the very best in town."

The contrast to our previous lodging was overwhelming. But this would have to suffice since we had no way to get anywhere else that day. Our after-dark activities could be talking, romanticizing or reading. Hopefully, Lee's six foot plus arm's-reach was enough to change the lightbulb high overhead. Otherwise, reading would not be an option.

Lee reassured Oki the room was fine. I quickly removed our sunscreen, camera and umbrella out of my pack, in case we needed them later. We then retraced our steps as Oki busily locked the many locks behind us. Maybe his fantasy was to be a jail warden. Anyway, he assured us that he would reopen everything when we returned.

We hiked off to explore our other lodging possibility, curious about the real advantage of staying with Oki. After walking a piece down the road and asking for directions, we approached a small house. Ascending some outside steps, we inspected our option. There were candles in the room. No electricity was available. A porcelain washbasin sat on a wooden box. Pillowless twin beds with graying sheets stood side by side. There was nothing else in the room but a noxious odor drifting in from the outhouse nearby. The price was minimal but Oki's was deluxe in comparison!

We thanked them for showing us the room and headed back to town for a beer and lunch. Our little thatched hut had now become a memory … today we were living in Benque.

Lee and I walked around looking for a place to eat. There were only a few streets with merchants to explore. We found one restaurant whose sign was a big chicken cut out of plywood hanging perpendicular to the front of the store. I hoped that the quality of food served was in no way related to the ugly chicken painted in red and green with a wattle way out of proportion to the rest of its face, but we saw no other choice.

The restaurant was empty except for the four older men playing cards at one of the tables. It was about noon, when did people eat? We sat down and waited for someone to come out of the kitchen. A rather young shy girl came out and I asked what they had. "Chicken," was the response.

"Anything else?" Lee asked.

"Rice," she said. "We have chicken and rice, but on Sunday we have beef, too."

The meal wasn't bad. The chicken had been simmered in some red sauce, and with the bread she gave us we spotlessly cleaned our plates. The coffee that accompanied our meal was instant (a jar of Nescafe sat on every table). There was no other coffee served even though the Guatemalan border was minutes away. Dawdling over our coffee, we waited for the onslaught of customers; hoping that the place would quickly become a hub of activity or that the men would look up from their cards or just some wee bit of entertainment would drift our way ... but this was not to be, so we walked out into the sun to explore our new environment.

Benque was a serious contrast to our idyllic setting in the jungle high above the Macal River. It was a small village on the Mopan River, and we began to feel what it was like to be a rural native of Belize. The sun was hot as we walked up and down the streets. We passed a small square with long brown grass and a few stone benches. It stood empty and across from a stucco Catholic Church. We peered in and that, too, was empty. The church stood waiting for the footsteps of the people—only the flickering flames of the vigil lights moved. Turning around and walking down the next street we heard a familiar voice.

"Oh friends, I am going back to San Ignacio why don't you go to the ruins? I need more riders in my car but the day is hot and no one else is traveling but the lady I bring to the city. Come along and see our Mayan kings. There is shade by the road for you to wait for me when you are finished."

We instantly agreed with his idea but asked Carlos if we had to pay for the empty seats. He laughed and said, "No, I will charge you like the car is full, but mostly important is that you see my country."

We climbed into the back seat. "This guy could make a fortune as a salesman," I whispered to Lee.

Smiling, Lee asked him about where we could eat in Benque.

"There are two places. One has the sign of a chicken on it. The other place is a house across from the church where Maria and her daughter serve food early in the morning until late in the afternoon. I will show you where it is when we come back."

Then he proceeded to tell the passenger in the front seat about how he had picked us up earlier in the day and spoke of us with such fervor that overhearing him I could have surmised that we were very dear friends.

Turning his head Carlos said, "Here we are. There is the ferry to the ruins. If you are thirsty while you are waiting for me, walk across the street and around the bend and there is a woman who sells cola in her house. You will know her house from the sign. Goodbye, my friends. I will return in an hour or so. Enjoy my country's ruins."

We were dropped across from a primitive hand-painted sign nailed to a tree by the ferry across the river. The board was white and the capital letters painted in black read "XUNANTUNICH." It seemed like the calendar had rolled back many years—the place could almost be anywhere and the time, "when things began." Only the sign gave away that the location was of Spanish descent.

Lee and I stood in the hot sun and watched the ferry coming across the river. There was shade on the other river bank from large overhanging trees. The navigator had been resting, but now we had arrived and it was his responsibility to pick us up.

The ferry was small approximately 20 by 15 feet. It was more of a raft with a fence around it. The most unusual thing about it was the mechanical means by which the ferry operated. It utilized only manpower ... and the fuel was calories from the person hand-drawing it across the river.

There was a cable on each side of the ferry to keep it in position. One heavy cable was attached to trees on the opposite sides of the river and acted as a guide so the ferry would not move down the river. The second cable was attached to two stationary supports, each containing a metal wheel so that by using a winch he could wind the cable onto the wheel in the direction that we were headed. It was so simple that it was humorous. The man who hand-drew that ferry felt pleased to have such an important task, telling us that he had done his job for ten years.

It was a short sixty feet across, but it was an enjoyable ride. He talked as he wound up the cable, happy to have an audience. We were his third customer that day; the others were a park- attendant and a guide.

He motioned ahead. "Follow the dirt path to the ruins. I will be here for you when you come back."

There was some shade from trees overhanging the dirt path, but the air was still and hot. We walked along realizing that we had not inquired how far it was and hoped it was a short distance. The river brush had been cleared to make a narrow path. I wondered how many visitors came through. The ferry was the only means to get to that side of the river. It didn't feel like they had much traffic to the ruins if they had three employees for the entire area!

We arrived at an opening. There was no one in sight, confirming the ferryman's census. Feeling the sun beating down with such strength also made me think there was a reason for the absence of others. What were we doing here in the heat of the day?

A young man appeared from nowhere, wearing a very large cowboy hat and an even larger smile. I'm sure he was very relieved that he now had some entertainment and possible income. He introduced himself as Bentley and said he was at our service and would give us a tour of the ruins for "no charge" but, of course, he would take donations later if we insisted.

Then he gave us another smile. "I am sure that you will be pleased with my tour," and led us across the field. Maybe visitors frequented here after all.

There were two excavations. The temple was close to the river and called El Castillo, which had been completely excavated. "However," Bentley said, "some big stones were taken for analyzing and that is why we use plaster castings." On one of the outside walls, white images of warriors and kings had been plastered on the buildings. The color and quality of the material chosen were quite a shock to the aesthetics of the pyramid. There must have been a reason for the apparent amateurish look but I doubted Bentley knew.

"Who has the real copies?" Lee asked.

"An American university ... I do not know where they live."

Realizing my hypothesis was now confirmed I decided to try a personal question. "How did you get such an interesting name?"

His large smile returned and he was eager to answer. "In San Ignacio, there is a military base of Englishmen. It has been there for many years but now they are leaving one by one. We have our independence, you know? My mother, she was pretty and very young. She worked selling cigarettes in the canteen and she meets Morris, my father. He is very young too but they are in love. They get married and he is trying to find a place for them in San Ignacio to live. But my mother, she is still living with her family in Benque so my father drives back and forth every day on his motorcycle. One night it rains and a truck does not see him. My father, he dies. I am still in my mother's stomach and I never see him."

"Did you ever meet anyone in his family?" I asked.

"No. My mother was sad until I was a little boy. Then I make her laugh because I look like my father and now she is happy because I marry in September. At church, I have a special place on the 'table for blessings' where my priest allows me to leave a photo of my father. Every day I light a candle and say a prayer for him."

"But how did you get your name?" I repeated.

"My father, he always talks about the car a rich uncle will give him after he gets done with the military. He always carried a picture to show my mother his Bentley car, saying they would return to England and drive around proudly feeling blessed at their good fortune. My mother, she knew my father, Morris, loved the Bentley and so named me. I know my father would have loved me very much. I will honor him by naming my first son Morris."

His story was ended and we walked to the top landing of the temple, a small stone mountain leading to the sun. Not a cloud was in sight; the sky had solidarity to it. The stone was so hot that I felt like I was standing on a bed of coals, I could see how the natives feared the Sun God!

Putting my umbrella up, I looked down at the river and tried to forget the heat. The river did make me feel cooler, as did watching the long green grass on both banks slightly moving and casting shadows on the water.

Many centuries ago the Mopan must have been a larger and deeper artery to meet the needs of the people. The temple was an artifact of those times. Presently, no human dwellings could be seen on our side. Across the river perched clumsily on stilts were the huts of today's inhabitants, but the flavor of antiquity remained. After slowly walking down the temple steps we approached the courtyard while Bentley gave us his interpretation of history; his hands continuously moved, accompanied by frequent smiles. My very favorite expression was when he would look contemplative and serious, then lifting his hat and scratching his head he would finally break into a beatific smile as though he were enlightened. His history lessons were "Bentley's Blend" of little fact and mostly fiction, but he was nonetheless an interesting respite.

He ended his discourse under a small pavilion that sheltered some larger stones protruding from the ground that questionably showed the image of a warrior. Under Bentley's tutelage, we were educated as to the exact outline of the image and convinced that the stones were of a disgraced warrior since they were not found in the temple. Why would we argue with him? Besides, it was cooler under the pavilion. So we just sat on the ground until Bentley finished his history lesson. Eventually, switching to his private life he told us about his fiancée, then repeated his admiration for his father.

Bentley finally ran out of stories and we felt ready to move along. The heat had abated and it was just time to leave. Generously tipping Bentley, we walked to the ferry. After crossing the river, Lee left to find the lady with the colas and I stayed, awaiting our driver. I reflected on the day's events and got side-tracked with wishing, wasn't there a way to make our trips longer? More than a glimpse would make it even more fascinating. Then I reprimanded myself for not feeling grateful for any experience. I was rescued by Lee carrying two clear plastic bags with orange pop in the bottom and a straw protruding from the tops.

Laughing, he handed me a bag, "Now I don't need to return the bottles."

The orange liquid and the coolness of the late afternoon were very palatable. It was comfortable waiting for our ride and watching the river flow past us. We decided to try and buy some hammocks and return to the peaceful spot.

Our taxi returned and took us to Benque. Driving by Maria's, we were shown the only other place to eat. Her house/restaurant sat on the river's edge and looked like an interesting possibility. With only the two places available we would inevitably try her food (especially now that it came recommended). Our driver let us out on the square by the church. After thanking and paying him, we went on our way.

In smaller villages, the best activity for us is to walk and observe, and find a seat from which to watch, whether it is in a restaurant or out in the open. The ideal situation is to have some exchange with the locals, yet, be aware that many are leery of foreigners. I thought about all the places our eyes and feet have wandered. Last year Lee and I traveled to Mexico City to visit the Aztec Teotihuacan ruins, Guanajuato to visit the mines and San Miguel de Allende for the markets. Mexico City was a dense and crazy-paced place and we both voted for smaller towns with less congestion and bustle. I admit that Benque fit the superlative category of our wish. I think Lee had the same thoughts as I did because he took my hand and said, "I'm glad we came here."

The physical activity revived us. The heat was gone and a breeze had come up. We probably appeared strange to the locals as we walked up and down the streets. Children greeted us with laughter before running into their homes. Many of the small wooden houses stood flush with the sidewalk: the double doors that opened to the street showed people sitting on simple chairs talking or watching a small television.

Sometimes, a woman or man stood leaning in the door frame oblivious to our presence. I wished that I'd had an invisible camera to photograph a particular small man with coal-black hair wearing a large white athletic shirt, rumpled khaki pants and rubber sandals, smoking a cigarette and looking into a space over our heads. He seemed unaware of the world before him and the bright aqua room behind him. Included in his photograph would be a large gold crucifix on the wall over a small table with a huge bouquet of bright red plastic flowers and a white ceramic figurine. There were steps in front of him and a small piece of metal roofing hung overhead—a shield from any rains should he decide to have a smoke in wet weather. His head didn't move as we walked by, his hand automatically went to his mouth for another puff on his cigarette ... his mind stayed far away.

We walked by houses on stilts and huts on grass-barren lots. Some yards had fences constructed with miscellaneous pieces of metal sheeting and wood, creating an impasse for anything small and lively: children, dogs, pigs and chickens. All horses and goats were tethered. Wash tubs and tables stood empty but clothes were still drying on lines or strewn over any available bush or fence. The maintenance duties of the day were done and it was time for dinner.

We could see pots outside over fires and smell savory aromas floating by. We felt timid in this village. It seemed like we were the only outsiders there. No one seemed hostile; maybe they were timid, too?

Passing by a large open door with tables and activity, we retraced our steps to explore all social possibilities. We found the establishment to be a local bar. The activity seemed centered around the two men playing pool. Lee and I chose a table with three views; the billiard game, the doorway and the bar. Unfortunately, no food was served. The jar of pickled eggs sitting on the bar did not look appealing, which left us with the only remaining choice of chips with our beer. Tomorrow we would go in search of fruit.

Maybe Oki would advise us where to find it.

The bartender came over with our beverages and asked us where we were from. "The U.S. Cleveland, Ohio," Lee said.

The man smiled. "Maybe you can show me where it is on the map over the bar." Turning toward the bar he proudly pointed to a 4 x 8 foot map hanging on the wall. "My nephew painted it for me."

It was reminiscent of the style of the chicken sign we had seen earlier that day; out of proportion and very stylized. The background was light blue and against it was a chain of green countries painted in an image not dissimilar to a wish rising out of Aladdin's lamp. A very large rendering of Belize took up two-thirds of the space and some wisps of land leading to and from were very incidental. The country's flag was painted on the bottom corner of the board. Many towns were labeled in Belize. The few green spots here and there I assumed were islands.

We sat for some time. Nobody came over and we didn't move from our chairs. The bartender brought us another round of chips and beer. We weren't excited about the nutritious diet, but we had to be versatile.

The billiard game was still being played when we left. A lean man in jeans and a dirty baseball hat seemed to be the hustler. Every time he played he won. The men seemed to be enjoying themselves. Neither of us could see the coins that were being put down for the bets. Hopefully, nobody went home penniless.

Walking back to Oki's, Lee and I discussed what to do about dinner. Maria's wasn't open except for breakfast and lunch and so that left the chicken place again or finding a grocery store. When Oki opened all of the doors to let us in the room we asked him how late the restaurant was open. "Always," he said. "The owner is very rich."

The chairs on the outer landing were occupied so there was no alternative to staying in our room unless we wanted to walk to the plaza. We were glad we brought a lightbulb so we could read if there was electricity. The contents of our small backpacks (about the size of an expanded briefcase) we had down to a science. This enabled us to walk around effortlessly without getting blisters on our backs. Our gear consisted of two shirts, two T-shirts, an umbrella, three pairs of underwear and three pairs of socks, plus shorts, a nylon jacket and a pair of pants, a bottle of shampoo, multivitamins, and a bottle of Advil for those nights of aching legs. And, a swimsuit, hat and sandals plus shoes we wore. In addition, we had small nylon bags folded in our packs so that we had another means to carry a few things around. Miscellaneous items: two blow-up neck pillows to allow better reading, flashlights, suntan lotion and insect repellent, 5-8 paperbacks to read and swap; two glasses and a bottle opener accompanied by two flasks of whisky for medicinal purposes. Oh, and Woolite (liquid laundry detergent) and a pair of 72-inch laces to hook together for a clothesline or cut down for shoes.

With some difficulty, Lee changed the high overhead bulb. Sitting with our backs to the wall we both became engrossed in our books and neglected the passing of time, Lee looked up and realized that it was dark outside our small window. Deciding it was time to try another meal at the Lucky Chicken, we locked our room and went down to the lobby. Lee was handing our key to Oki when all the lights went out. We stood together in the dark as Oki started shouting at the boys buying Cokes, "Get out! Get out! I don't want any stealing. Come back tomorrow." He shooed everyone away so quickly that we were still standing in the same spot after the place had emptied.

"Is the restaurant open without electric?" I asked.

"No, when the electric goes off at this hour that means we will not have it back until tomorrow."

"Why?"

"Soon everyone will be in bed so candles and flashlights are all you need. Just wait until I lock the store and I will escort you to my friend who sells food from her house."

Lee and I sat out on the front step and waited. Soon Oki appeared with a very long silver flashlight. Directing the light he said, "Follow me."

Our flashlights were upstairs behind dark doors. With a sliver of a moon and Oki as our guide, we went in search of food. We took a right, then a left, walked a few blocks and turned right again. Were we walking in circles or was it my imagination? Finally, Oki stopped in front of a house. "Let me see what she has today," he said.

A minute later he came back out. "She has biscuits and bananas."

"Great," Lee said, "we'll have eight biscuits and four bananas."

"She only has six biscuits and three bananas left."

"What about you?" Lee asked.

"I've eaten so you can have everything."

He came back with a brown bag. Then we followed our leader home.

After Oki sold us two Cokes, he led us up the two flights of stairs holding the long silver flashlight in one hand and an unlit candle and matches in the other. Then he opened our room and waited until we found our flashlights.

"Where are the other guests?" I asked.

"You are the only two this evening."

"But I thought that I saw two people sitting in the chairs earlier this evening."

"You did, but they are border guards who went to work."

So, we lit our candle, grabbed our pillows and food and flask, and pulled the chairs from the inside through a door onto a small porch two floors above Oki's front entrance where we could look out into the night. We opened our brown bag for dinner.

After eating our bananas, we divided the six biscuits (which were like hot crossed buns covered with pink frosting) and poured ourselves a glass of Coke and whisky. While slowly eating our biscuits, Lee and I chatted, looking up at a sliver of a moon and sometimes down at the street covered in darkness. Eventually, talked out and tired, we went to bed.

It was easy to sleep. We were both exhausted from our long day. Benque was quiet with the early "lights out" and I would have slept forever except for the persistent feeling that something was walking on my skin. I lay quietly wondering if my imagination had reared its head, or actual insects were marching in a parade across my body. Lee lay by my side snoring … nothing was bothering him!

Remembering the flashlight under my pillow, I turned it on. It was pretty difficult to see anything in that light. Finally, I sat up and held the flashlight in one spot, and watched. Some small tiny bugs were indeed moving over our bedsheets and my legs to some unknown destination.

Lee awoke with my movements muttering, "What are you doing?"

"There is some kind of bugs bothering me."

There was a delay before his response. "I thought I was dreaming that something was crawling on my skin."

Both of us watched these black dots walking across our sheets. "Didn't we bring some super concentrated Cutter's lotion with us?" I asked.

Putting drops of Cutter's on our skin and sheets, we smeared the stuff around as far as it would go. Then we lay waiting, rather, I waited. Lee had already fallen back to sleep. No little black bugs were seen or felt. They must have found a detour with all our commotion.

It seemed very early when noise woke us up. The clock read 6 a.m., and as the minutes passed the volume of street noise increased.

"We may as well get up," said Lee. "Besides, I'm starved. I hope Maria's is open."

"Hopefully, we can find some other fruit today. Living off of starch and sodas isn't my idea of a good diet," I said.

We were out of there in a few minutes. Since our room just had a toilet, neither of us felt dirty enough to try the shower stalls across the hall. Maybe later we could find a place on the river bank where we could swim.

Oki was very chipper, and as he took our key inquired if we slept well. Somehow mentioning tiny visitors didn't seem appropriate, especially having seen our other option. After all, he was doing his best; both the room and sheets appeared clean. Neither of us said anything except to ask if Maria's were open.

"What does she serve for breakfast?" I asked.

"She serves beans and rice and eggs for breakfast and her soup for lunch," Oki replied.

"That's it?"

"The soup she changes every day but breakfast is always the same."

"Any place we can get fruit around here?"

Oki explained a few places to try in addition to the lady we bought the bananas from last night.

While walking over to eat, we saw that the square was deserted except for the people walking in and out of the church. The women all wore mantillas or small doilies on their heads. The men removed their hats and after crossing themselves dropped their heads and walked respectfully into the building. Nearby a horse and colt stood waiting for their master or mistress to return. Two cars were parked down the side street.

Across the square, we entered Maria's. A few tables were occupied. One man was using his bread to clean his plate. It looked like he enjoyed it!

The waitress cheerfully took our order and returned with two fried eggs, rice and beans; all sharing the same plate and accompanied by two slices of white bread and Nescafe coffee. I asked her if the milk in the pitcher was pasteurized. Hoping she understood my question when she answered, "Yes." I dumped a healthy amount into my coffee.

The breakfast, our only choice in town, did not meet our nutritional needs but we did enjoy watching the other customers. They looked well nourished. Maybe it was just my Scandinavian metabolism that needed more! "Let's just scope out any shop we see and maybe we'll find something to eat. It'll be our exercise for the morning," I said to Lee.

After having another cup of coffee, we left to walk around. It was still very early but the entire population was out and about. Some people acknowledged us; others did not. We kept wandering the same streets as before hoping for some miracle, like a small food store to magically appear. We asked a few people and could get only one response and that there was a place "coming into" town. Finally, we found a small store that sold canned goods, and bananas and had crates of eggs piled high upon the counter. The milk was in boxes and so were the juices. We looked around. I asked the owner where the oranges were and he told us about a stand a few more blocks away. Also, we asked about fresh baked goods and were told about the same lady we got the biscuits from last evening.

We chose some bananas, a large cellophane package of coconut cookies and some Jif peanut butter made in the United States and priced according to the huge import tax ... and off we went to look for the oranges.

We saw the stand ahead, unattended and locked up with a huge padlock. Sitting on the two stumps alongside the stand, we waited for someone to walk by.

It was a nice morning and Lee and I were fed and had nothing to do so we waited. There was activity further down the street so we just watched the people moving around and knew that they would come our way. Someone finally did and was friendly enough to answer Lee's question. "He goes to San Ignacio to the market and should be back anytime."

Taking out our books we continued to wait. Time evaporated and before long a taxi drove up. "My friends, I see you again. How are you?" Getting out of the car, Carlos shook our hands. Walking around to the passenger waiting by the trunk, he told him of his new American friends.

I was beginning to feel that the villagers must need "Carlos the taxi driver" to tell stories and make them laugh or maybe the truth was that we needed him. He talked on and on while helping the merchant unload his fruit and bread and sweets, telling him about bringing us to Benque and showing us around and then bringing us to the ruins and back. He was totally enamored with his tale and was out of breath when he finished. Then he turned to us and said, "This is my brother Emo. He will sell you only the best fruit."

Emo shook Lee's hand and welcomed him, ignoring me, but that was OK. I sat back down on the stump and Lee purchased an orange and four biscuits (to be used with the Jif later). Then, peeling the orange he handed me a slice and we sat happily eating and watched as the people came out of nowhere and approached the stand. Emo and his brother talked to the consumers loudly enough for us to repeatedly hear the same story. People looked over and smiled. We nodded in return but felt time to leave since no one had ventured over to converse. As we walked off, Carlos waved. "See you later," he said.

Lee and I headed for the river to look for a place to swim. It was a beautiful morning and there was action everywhere. Women were washing clothes while their children were entertained splashing, swimming and playing.

Seeing a tree with a huge broken limb at the water's edge, Lee said, "Let's go over there and sit. We won't be too conspicuous and the tree will shelter us from the sun." Lee and I stationed ourselves on the limb with our backs against the tree and watched the day's events.

We were so preoccupied with the activity that we sat there most of the day. Our only clock was the travel alarm which lay on the floor of our hotel room so we were unaware of the time passing. We ate our biscuits and oranges then read a little and watched the kids and moms hour after hour.

The highlight of our day was a man who rode up on his horse and trotted right into the water, a deep part, so that the horse had to swim. The horse swam for a minute and went for the other side. After turning around on the riverbank the horse stood looking across the water, his master still astride, then walked into the water and swam back. This apparently was not an uncommon sight, because no one except Lee and I lifted their heads.

To us, it seemed a bizarre spectacle to observe this large caramel-colored horse with a white mane, and a small Mestizo man on his back, appear on the scene and cross the river twice. The finale was when the horse stopped as he arrived on our shore and waited as if "on cue" while the rider took off each boot and emptied it of water. And they galloped off to resume their daily tasks.

Feeling inclined to swim, we took turns going back to the hotel to put on our swimsuits. Since our big branch on the river was a prime spot we could not assume it would be there if we both left at the same time.

Lee and I had become fixtures. Three little boys started swimming in front of us and after showing off for a few minutes, ignored us and started to play among themselves. Their intrigue was a new toy; a pair of goggles. They took turns wearing them and swimming below the surface, excitedly coming up for air and sending the next child down. Nobody was a bully and they had a wonderful time.

Finally, in the late afternoon, we walked upstream and went swimming in a more private area. The mothers and children were gone and teenagers had replaced them, flirting amongst themselves and passing a cigarette back and forth.

The water was cool and delicious. The sun had moved away from the earth making the air feel gentle. Staying in the water made us refreshed and ready for a change of pace. Deciding that plenty of daylight remained, this would be the perfect opportunity to walk to the Guatemalan border. Maybe we could cross and buy some good coffee. If nothing else our bodies would be exercised and sleep would come easy at Oki's.

Walking down the road was exactly what we needed after our idle hours on the riverbank. Changing into our slacks and hiking shoes, we carried a small pack with our oranges and camera and, of course, our passports if we were to cross the border. There was little activity at the end of the day and we walked uninterrupted except for a few cars and trucks. A large dog, chained to a post furiously barked as we passed.

The houses became sparser the further away we walked from Benque. Most of the dwellings which sat on the landscape were constructed very primitively; the distance from town probably made the property less desirable and inexpensive.

Lee and I chatted as we walked the two miles to the border. "You know," I said, "I wish you had come with me in 1979 when I visited the Mayan Ruins at Tikal. We had just met and you weren't about to drop the bucks to come— and I wasn't about to treat you!"

Lee laughed and put his arm around me. "Then I would've been a kept man."

"Ha-ha," I answered. "But even with you as my bodyguard, it wouldn't have been safe. Remember, I had to spend a fortune to go with a tour group because of all the unrest." Civil war had started in 1960 and had never stopped. A military junta remained relentless in their acts of genocide against the Mayan community. Anyone was at risk ... and still was ....

We arrived at the guard station and began explaining in Pidgin Spanish our desire to walk across the river into Guatemala. There was a store across the bridge that Oki told us to visit. We assured them that we would return within the hour. The guards were concerned that we not travel into Guatemala alone since the guerillas were not hesitant to bother foreigners.

We couldn't help but ask about our friend Mick who we had socialized with during our stay in the thatched huts. The guards seemed to be fond of him but when they asked, "Who was he with this time?" we realized that his interest in women was not just restricted to Mindy!

It felt strange walking over a bridge into another country. Especially when a significant number of Guatemalan soldiers were marching back and forth with guns resting upon their backs! We looked straight ahead and walked into the store. It was an old-fashioned general store. The young female clerk was quite shy, especially when we tried our Spanish. Pointing seemed to work a lot better. Lee and I each bought ourselves a hammock plus two pounds of the good Guatemalan coffee. I also bought a small flat tin of Nivea cream because the container was so unique. We walked up the street a few blocks, but with the somber soldiers roaming around, our inquisitive spirits were dampened.

Shortly, we were back at the border station having our passports stamped again. The guards thought we were pretty amusing just to walk in and out of Guatemala. Lee and I smiled at their spirit of humor and then walked off carrying our hammocks under our arms.

When we arrived back at our hotel, Oki gave us a big smile and asked, "How do you like my country?"

Lee assured him it was wonderful and asked if the Magic Chicken was serving dinner yet.

"Oh, yes," answered Oki, "they serve dinner all day."

"But when do they eat dinner?" I asked, hoping to catch the hour of peak activity.

"Any time they are hungry," he answered.

I laughed to myself. His wit reminded me of my Midwestern Scandinavian relatives!

Lee and I went up to our room. It felt quite stuffy. After opening our window we sat in the lobby looking out at the traffic, discussing when to eat dinner. We were famished but since it was our evening's activity we also wished to have company while we ate, just for the atmosphere.

Deciding to wait a little longer, Lee purchased a coke from Oki and we ate a few coconut cookies while watching the people below walk in and out of our view. Some were in a hurry, especially those with large packages balanced on their shoulders. The majority seemed immersed in social activity; talking, walking and stopping to explain, sometimes laughing and then disappearing from our frame. It was the same feeling I had when we rode the bus and watched people pass by outside our window.

Finally, it was time. The street seemed to quiet down—where else could everyone be but eating? So off we went to the Magic Chicken.

Our instincts were right! Many tables were filled. We casually walked by, scanning the plates for possible choices. When we sat down we knew our one choice since it was all we saw.

Lee and I ate our chicken and rice and bread along with the others. The atmosphere was friendly; people were talking among themselves. The families dining that evening consisted of well-mannered children eagerly eating their chicken.

The restaurant sat on a corner, and the painted chicken sign stood on the main street. There were roll-up doors on both the side street and the front that allowed a nice breeze to wander through the restaurant. We reminded each other that here we were in this temperate climate in the middle of winter. Lee and I sat absorbing the sights and smells, discussing our plans for tomorrow; whether we should stay another day or go to San Ignacio for a few days. The city stood high on a hill where two rivers joined. Maybe we could find a place to tie our hammocks and watch the water and read a book?

We left the Magic Chicken and walked down the middle of dimly lit streets following the example of those ahead of us. Maybe walking in the center of the road was a declaration of a curfew for motor vehicles and traffic. It made the town quiet and peaceful. Everyone was languidly finishing the day and we felt part of it.

The electricity didn't go out that night. The music below us kept us informed of that. I never asked Oki if he made much money with his tapes and colas. But I know he kept busy.

There was one other occupant in the hotel. I think our bed bugs moved on to his room because we didn't feel them again. Of course, we put Cutter's lotion on before we went to bed so they may have just walked around us. But then we were exhausted after our rigorous day on the river.

The music continued to play as we slept. When Oki pulled his metal door down, we didn't hear that either. We were asleep in our Belizean bed, oblivious to all terrestrial sounds.

CHAPTER FOUR

San Ignacio

A wakened by the early morning street traffic, I lay waiting for Lee to move or open his eyes. Maybe he was thinking, as I was, "Where do we eat this morning?" Those primal senses never disappear. I felt snobbish lying there wishing for something palatable when it was such a luxury to be visiting a unique place and be comfortable. We had traveled in other countries where we had felt hostility and discomfort. The lack of breakfast options was beginning to feel more ludicrous the more I thought about it.

I heard a sleepy voice next to me say, "Why don't we leave for San Ignacio now? It probably would be easy to get a ride in that direction. We could have an orange and wait for coffee until later."

Soon we were walking down the street and past the church. I recognized the horse and colt standing precisely where they were yesterday. Only today, the mare wore a red and yellow plaid blanket. She probably was thinking about her lucky fortune; their owner was religious and here they stood waiting instead of working.

I turned around and looked once again, Benque looked so peaceful. They were isolated from any major traffic. How many more years would "the town" retain this identity? Maybe the residents hungered for the technological wizardry that was available in the world or maybe the sleepy town would be "discovered" and thereafter be inscribed on all the maps of the tourist world.

Arriving at the edge of town we waited for a ride to San Ignacio. Assuming that our infamous taxi driver would drive up, we were totally surprised when another car stopped and asked where we were going. He was not as loquacious as Carlos, but spoke a few words to the other passengers about the price of petrol and commented on the marriage of someone's son. I looked out the window and wondered where we would be staying that night. The scenery was lush and quiet, the river on one side and the houses on the other. They blended into one another: primitive and functional as they had been for the last umpteen years.

Approaching the town I noticed a large, modest building sitting upon a hill. I whispered to Lee, "Let's stop here and see what it is. Maybe it's a hotel."

The driver overheard and said. "This is the San Ignacio Hotel. Do you want to get out?"

The lobby was silent, but a young woman, sitting by a desk, looked up and welcomed us. "Can I help you?"

We asked to look at a room. The hotel was one floor with a

small restaurant and bar adjoining the lobby. The lodging was to the left. I noticed a few people eating breakfast. Lee and I looked at each other with relief. The hotel clerk walked down the hall. We followed her to look at our options.

The rooms facing the entrance were less interesting than those at the back. We chose a back corner room. It faced the valley overlooking the town. A small door allowed access to two wooden chairs outside, an ideal spot to watch the sun come and go. Lee left with the clerk to pay in advance. I remained seated in one of the chairs outside and loudly whispered to myself, "Yes, yes! We've found another wonderful spot."

Upon Lee's return, we immediately went for breakfast. Sitting close to one of the windows, the view overlooking the valley was very beautiful. And today our food was better: the bread was toasted; the beans and eggs remained the same. However, to our delight, the meal was served with real coffee!

After our second cup, we voted to take showers and set off to explore, knowing that when the afternoon heat descended upon us our ambition would dissipate and our curiosity wane.

Walking down the nearest road, three girls were approaching wearing wet clothes and combing wet hair. They were laughing among themselves as if they had just pulled "a fast one." Shortly, out of the brush along the road, came two wet and very unhappy young boys. Somehow they must have been the brunt of the joke. They were complaining to one another. When they saw the girls ahead, they ran after them. We turned off the road through the brush to follow the boys' footsteps down a very narrow and steep path, and "voila" we came upon the river.

"Fantastic," said Lee. "Maybe we can hang our hammocks later in the day and relax."

Looking around, there were not any trees large enough to use our hammocks, but there was enough brush to find shade. We agreed to return later and spend the afternoon.

Hiking up the same path we decided to walk into town. Everything should be open because it was still morning and people would be doing their shopping. Approaching the main square I could see a man sitting on the ground next to a tree wearing a plaid gingham shirt, shorts and tennis shoes. He spoke to us as we walked by, "Hey, where are you from?" Pausing, he threw the question into the air and then quickly answered himself. "I'm from Eden Prairie, Minnesota. Know anyone there?"

We stopped in our tracks. "Minnesota," I responded. "I was born and raised in Willmar and Minneapolis. What brings you here?"

He stood up and extended his hand. "Hello, I'm Rev. Ted Sandstrom. I retired from the Baptist ministry five years ago and every winter since I've come down here for three months. It's a friendly place, and it's very cheap too." Then he laughed at the sound of his words.

"Where do you stay and what do you do with your time?" Lee asked.

I watched as Rev. Ted answered the question. He spoke easily and seemed to find himself humorous. His stature was quite small, maybe 140-50 pounds and scrawny. His hair was gray and his face was nicely aged. He wore heavy tortoise-rimmed glasses which were turning white from the years in contact with his warm skin. Ted either needed sunglasses or a new prescription because he squinted as he looked at us.

"The best place to stay is above the police station. I looked around plenty to make my find. It's only three dollars a night and you just can't beat it! The room is clean and there's a shower stall with hot water down the hall that I can use. The rooms were for any overflow necessary for the jail; they never used it so they decided to rent it out."

This is amazing, I thought to myself; the austerity that a person will take on to save a nickel. We did a fair amount of it ourselves, but this guy was the champion, hands down. "Is there a chair in lobby or light to read by?" I asked, hoping that Ted would find time to read in the three months that he visited San Ignacio.

"Oh yes," he replied. "There is a small desk and chair. I borrowed a lamp so I could keep a journal and read my Bible. I stay very active. There is a Methodist church down the street that keeps me quite busy and then I help the locals harvest. Right now I am waiting for a truck that will take a group of us to a plantain orchard. I won't work hard but I will receive a little money which helps me with my expenses."

"But Rev. Ted," I asked, "don't Baptists pay any pension?"

"Yes, they do, but I'm giving money to the old folks' home that is caring for my mother. I am responsible for her since I'm her only child and my father long ago went to his due reward."

I considered asking exactly what his father's "due reward" was, but felt he might turn religious on me. Lee came to our rescue by posing another question. "Where do you eat around here?"

Back to the basics, I thought. However, by the looks of Rev. Ted, he was not going to help us in our quest for a good meal. Sure enough, my thoughts proved accurate.

"Well, usually I buy fruit and bread in the market for breakfast. In the evening I share a meal with the family of the woman who cleans the jail. She charges very little and it is a treat to be with her family." He looked down the street. "Here's my ride. Maybe I'll see you around town. Enjoy yourselves and pray for me that I will live longer than my mother." Then he got into the back of the truck and was gone down the street.

"What do you suppose he meant by that?" Lee asked.

"Either that he feared for his mother's future without his financial or emotional support, or that he wanted to live in a little luxury and spend his pension on himself."

"It seemed like he was enjoying himself anyway. Maybe he thinks of himself as some religious ascetic."

Rev. Ted's comments kept me occupied as we walked into town. Nothing had changed since arriving last week. The little grocery stood at the top of the hill. Lee and I kept walking and headed for the center of town. A store was open that displayed miscellaneous goods; we walked in to browse. A young girl worked the counter. "Can I help you?"

Lee asked if there were any merchandise made by Belizeans. We needed a few small gifts and any products in the food or crafts area would suffice. "We gather our fruits and vegetables," the girl said.

"But is there anything at all which has a label on it that says 'made in Belize'? We'd like to bring our friends gifts native to your land."

After much discussion, the only item that we came up with was beer made in Belize. Not a practical item to carry in our backpacks. Our sales girl knew of only one other option and sent us to a craftsman down the street who made things in wood.

We were excited at the prospect of something original. The shopkeeper was helpful and hospitable. The only problem: his trade was making furniture and nothing smaller. Sympathizing with our dilemma, he could not give us any new ideas.

I figured out a practical solution. "How about we send postcards from a Belizean post office using their stamps?" We weren't cheapskates but there seemed no alternative!

Since it was a wonderfully warm (not hot) and nice morning we decided our goal was to walk up and down each street and look for a place to dine later that evening. Lee kept muttering, "This is absurd. There's a bakery, bars and a dry goods store but no eateries." We stopped and questioned any person we felt comfortable asking. They told us of the taverns; maybe the town could not support a place where families would eat. We kept walking and asking. After all, it was a beautiful day! Finally, we turned onto a street and noticed a storefront with a sign hand-written in Chinese letters. The lower line said, "Restaurant." To our disappointment, the place did not appear open. We pounded on the door with no results. We even went around to the back, but finding no one, had just started to walk away when a small woman carrying a baby came out of a door nearby asking, "Can I help you?"

"Do you know when the restaurant is open?" I asked.

"Five o'clock."

"How long does it stay open?" Lee asked.

"'Til no one comes."

Thanking her, we left deciding to check the morning activity by the river, but this time we headed in the other direction, away from the town. We followed it to a wider and deeper area and sat on a log by the water. We could still see the women on the San Ignacio shores, beating clothes and using a washboard while their children played nearby. Lee got up and walked across the road to a neighboring bar and bought us a beer. "It sure is peaceful here," he said handing me a bottle. "I wonder how both of us love the water so much and what that means?"

"I don't know but let's toast to us."

We sat and looked at the river in silence and then I

started to laugh.

"What are you laughing at?"

"Your love for water and your creativity ... how you bought that Sunfish (very small sailboat) at the Red Cross auction last summer for $50 and fixed it up, found a woman to sew a new sail, and got out on the water. And you even rigged up a system in the back of the pickup to haul it."

"No, it's both of us, sweetheart. You saw the ad for the Red Cross Sailing lessons."

I interrupted. "But the funniest part was that we needed to show proof that we passed swimming with Red Cross and since I never did and didn't have a card like you, I gave Don's name (brother) as my instructor to verify my ability. And when I told him he was furious and said, 'What if they call me?'"

Lee chuckled and kissed my cheek. "Well, we both got our licenses to sail and here we are," he said, lifting his bottle in a toast.

We continued to sit by the river until the sun beat down from overhead reminding us and the women upstream to go elsewhere. A few remained but waded to areas with some shade. The rest meandered up the hill, baskets on their head, children following behind. We watched them disappear up onto the road. Soon Lee and I followed their example and walked back to our hotel, purchasing some fruit along the way. It was such a pleasure to arrive at our room with the outside chairs and view; we sat spoiling ourselves for a few luxurious moments and viewed our town.

Finally, we put our swimsuits on. Taking our towels and an umbrella, we headed for the beach, carefully walking down the steep decline of the hill until we arrived by the water.

Lee, looking around, walked out of my view.

"Judi," I heard in the distance, "I think I've found us a spot."

I ran to his voice down the river. He had found a private place where the shade would keep my fair skin from frying and where we could see any activity upriver, where the sandy beach looked grand and the swimming appeared to be.

Sitting on our towels and opening our books, we read and watched the water move by. It's difficult to know how long the river entertained us. Time just goes from one hour to the next. We monitored our time by changes: cool, hot, or dark.

All of a sudden we heard some commotion as a group of people dressed for a party arrived on the water's edge. There were men, women and children, plus two striking and very noticeable blond Englishmen in white vestments. (Belize is a melting pot of Mestizo, Creole and Garifuna with only a small population of white/Asian people). We did not make a sound but watched in anticipation. No one acknowledged our presence, but I am sure that they saw us; we must have appeared innocuous.

Shortly we found ourselves observing a river baptism. Everyone left their shoes on shore, and walked into the river singing and holding their Bibles. When the water was up to their knees they stopped walking (but not singing), swaying to the music and carrying on like something was supposed to happen. It did ... one minister prayed while the other minister read scripture; a few continued to hum in the background. Each minister and his recruit walked into deeper water until it was possible to submerge the "victim" by dunking her into the water. Two women were baptized: one sputtered when she came up, and the other was reverent and teary-eyed.

Even though the people were dressed in fancy clothes, it felt rather "tribal," like a rite of passage of some sort. Here was a group of people with skin of burnished gold to black in dramatic contrast to the blond Englishmen in white robes. It felt as if we were transported to a movie set from the 1950s. The religious event then took an unexpected turn when the congregation walked up the hill and the two clergymen stayed behind.

Suddenly, a camera magically appeared in the hands of one of the clergy and they begin laughing and taking pictures saying, "They won't believe it at home." It looked comical to see them posing, holding a Bible in one hand and looking very serious while extending the other hand in blessing with their eyes closed in prayer. I wanted to jump up and yell, "Hello," to see if they would drop their Bible in the river.

Within a few moments, the two men followed their flock up the embankment.

After seeing the religious production, the rest of the afternoon was anticlimactic. People came and went. They swam and played in the water but we sat books-in-hand hardly aware of their presence. Eventually, we took a swim after everyone had gone. We wanted to remain invisible. Keeping our Ivory soap floating by our side, we washed our hair ... with no one around we could now suds up. The water felt cool and delightful after walking around and sitting in the sand. Refreshed, we retraced our steps and went to our room to put on clean clothes and return to the Chinese restaurant for dinner.

Much to our delight, it was open. Another couple was already seated and awaiting their order. The cook had two black steel burners sitting on a table and attached to a full-sized propane tank. A wok sat on each burner and was filled with the ingredients that the customers ordered. When he finished, he served the dishes. (I believe the dishwasher was the woman who spoke to us earlier.)

Our cook told us the specials were a fish or chicken dish. Lee and I each chose one and watched the man as he cooked, ran in and out of the kitchen to get ingredients, or stopped to talk intermittently to the other couple who sat close to his cooking station. And the cook hummed to himself if there was a quiet moment. We just sat observing. It was such a pleasure to eat such excellent food and drink good tea, that we asked him if he would be open tomorrow night.

With full stomachs, we walked around the town digesting our food and perusing the same streets and homes as earlier that day. Walking by the church and looking in (since the door was open) we saw my fellow Minnesotan sitting by the aisle in one of the pews and having a jolly old time. He was singing at the top of his lungs with the congregation. His clothes were the same but looked a little disheveled from his activities earlier that day. (I hoped he had washed between activities so his neighbors were aware of his presence from his enthusiasm only.)

Making our way back to the hotel, we arrived and were greeted by an English couple standing by the bar watching for someone to walk through the front door. "Hello," the woman said."Come over and join us for a drink. We have a wonderful bottle of rum we just purchased and would like to make a toast to our future."

Lee looked over his shoulder and turning back muttered under his breath, "I guess she means us."

We walked over smiling, wondering if she were so loaded that she mistook us for someone else and if not, what she meant by "our future."

I will always remember Ivan and Eva and their infectious enthusiasm. We touched glasses, cheered them on, and toasted again. They were so excited over their new purchase of land where they would be starting a cacao bean farm. Their exuberance was at its best because this was the day that they had signed the papers. The property was now in their hands ... their agricultural adventure was finally to begin!

Ivan had been employed by the English government in the Department of Agriculture and had come over to consult on a few projects and had stumbled on a beautiful plot of land. He went back home and came up with the money. Eva chimed in at that point. "He's got the brains and I've got the bucks." She laughed at her joke and then added they were both hard workers and this would be their legacy. She, the talker of the two, said that after the acreage was cultivated and their house was built, they would start a family. Meanwhile, tomorrow they were going to set up two large canvas tents, one to sleep in and one to cook and serve the workers their meals. They both looked eager and healthy. After they regaled us about their history and their future events, we were running out of things to talk about. Lee and I realized they were ecstatic about their new beginning, but we had thought of all the questions we could muster. Fortunately, another couple walked into the bar and immediately was assimilated into the conversation. We graciously exited and wished Ivan and Eva the best. Now they could begin their story anew.

Back in our room, we sat on our patio and propped our feet on a stool, feeling lucky to have such a beautiful view below. The sky sparkled with stars. The air was filled with contentment.

We were awakened by someone ringing a church bell. I looked at the clock. It was 7 a.m.; was it Sunday? Why were they ringing it so early? Both of us got out of bed and decided to go to breakfast. We were thrilled at the prospect of having good coffee with our meal and remained at the hotel to eat. We talked while sipping our coffee. Lee had a wonderful idea. "Why not take our hammocks and catch a cab towards Benque? I remember seeing a lot of trees on the river bank and we could just hang our hammocks, read a book and watch the country life."

After packing up our hammocks, books and some cookies we were soon on the road, waiting for a cab. Within a short time we were riding along, Lee looking for the ideal spot. The cab driver found his actions amusing but slowed down as Lee looked at the trees and areas of shade and finally said, "Let us off."

It was a wonderful spot. The river ran past us toward the city ... there was an urgency to the water as it skimmed and slid over the rocks, sometimes billowing up in delight as it made small white waves over the rocks before spilling back into the river. As Lee and I lay reading and dreaming, watching the world around us, we were invisible from the world above and lost in the surroundings of the valley below.

Our time was heavenly. Lee waded in to swim upstream and floated on his back down the river where I lay reading. I, not as comfortable in the water, stayed closer to our site, swimming and wading across the river to explore. I found trees and woods but not any trails. Lee joined me and started skipping stones. He was the world's best stone-skipper; he had been raised on the Chemung River near Corning, New York, and spent endless hours perfecting his skill as well as his swimming. Lee swam like a fish. Being the youngest of six and living alone with his parents, he was very self-sufficient and had taught himself to swim rather than sink.

A few small children appeared from the other side of the road, saying nothing but chewing on their fingers and looking at us while watching Lee skip the stones. They finally ran off squealing, never to return. The most bizarre moment was when a huge black pig came ambling over to visit. He appeared to have a dorsal fin of fur on his back. We were reading but stopped to watch. He snorted along and came up to our hammocks and just looked at us. We assumed he was some strange mutant stock or a Belizean pig. Later, when I was reading about the local wildlife, I discovered it could have been a mammal called a peccary, a native wild species that resembles a razorback hog.

The day just passed, the momentum broken by our swims and the beverages we purchased by walking across the road and finding the local home outlet. It was a day of leisure! Time was peaceful and still. But Lee and I were aware that the spell would soon be broken since our visit to this idyllic place would be ending and we must return to Belize City.

Finally, our hunger dictated that day had moved by us. We had finished our books, eaten our cookies and the sun was no longer baking when we took our last swim. Walking up to the road, our hammocks under our arms, we stood waiting for a cab. We then realized that we had whiled away the time and were stranded. "This is great!" I said to Lee. "Here we sit mesmerized by the river and now we have an hour walk back to our hotel. Maybe we need a watch."

We walked on the road's edge, turning at the sound of any vehicle and putting out our thumbs for a ride. Finally, a man and woman stopped and offered us the back seat of a big white Fairlane Ford. They were coming from Guatemala and on their way to Cancun; a young college couple who drove down from Texas to see the country. The ride was short and the information we gleaned was limited, but I always smile at the memory of two Americans picking us up in the middle of nowhere in their huge white car.

Arriving back at the hotel, we dropped our gear and headed down the hill to our Chinese restaurant. The place was hopping:

we were the last table to be seated and the last to be served.

A couple sitting near us inquired how we were enjoying our visit. Answering I said, "I love the variety of people in your culture but most of all I love the feeling of the vegetation."

Lee replied, "The rivers are my favorite."

With our appetites satisfied we walked back up the hill seeking our deck chairs, conversation, and the open air. The lights went on in the city below. We looked at the sky above.

"Look over there," Lee said.

Excitedly we acknowledged the star as it shot into the air, then its trajectory moved towards the earth, and finally, the star fell out of view onto the ground ... both the star and we had a similar fortune landing in these unknown places.

Lee and I made a toast to a life of further exploration and then watched the shades-of-night being drawn.

The lights flickered on in the dwellings below. I wondered about Rev. Ted from Minnesota living over the jail and wished for him a very long life.

We sat comfortably; talking and watching the day spend its last hours. Eventually, all illumination was "snuffed" out like candles at a festival of lights ...

1990

Guyana

~∂

Two roads diverged in a wood, and I—
I took the one less traveled by,
And that has made all the difference.

—Robert Frost
The Road Not Taken

CHAPTER ONE

Georgetown

"Guyana? That's a crazy place to go. I wouldn't go back. "It was a jungle ... all I remember was the body bags I had to fill, the reports that I had to make out and the sadness I felt from the destruction of human lives. I was in the military at the time, in California, and they assigned us to Jim Jones's camp. What a mess it was. Some were identifiable, others were not. I'll never forget it." Those were the comments from the officer on the beat, on the street by our gallery in Cleveland Heights, Ohio.

Yes, the story was horrific and most people still associated Guyana with the cult of Jim Jones, who chose to test the love of his Jonestown followers by asking them to drink a lemonade containing cyanide. All 908 members—men, women, and children—obediently did. All ceased to breathe, and twelve years later, the event still lingered in all of our minds.

Nevertheless, the country appealed to us, or I should say to me, since I was the eager traveler. Lee and I had been together for almost ten years. We had left our corporate jobs and adjusted our lifestyle. Yes, the art gallery and frame shop was making a few dollars after eight years, but we took additional measures to ensure its success and future. We owned two duplexes, sold one and moved to the other after rehabbing the third floor to live rent-free. Also, we had purchased a dilapidated cabin on the lot next to our screen house; a screened-in-pavilion with low walls and a door. Lee and I had repaired the cabin and installed a wood stove giving us the option of spending weekends year-round. We loved the outdoors, took walks, and raised our dog, Sunshine. Lee had started taking classes in sculpture, using hardened clay (a lifelong dream of his). A ceramic engineer graduate, his life had been more practical until now. Our passion for each other was mutual, but added to my list were the gallery, travel and writing. As far as travel destinations, Lee didn't care where we went. I did the research, looked in our file cabinet under "T" for travel (where I collected cash) to see what the budget was, and decided. Of course, Lee gave his input, but our goal was to fly somewhere out of the country to a warm place during Cleveland's cold season when the snow was ten inches deep. We backpacked and were very frugal, enabling us to go further away. This year we looked at Venezuela, but there was some trouble there. Next, we were on our way to Peru. But the Peruvian embassy said, "Don't go alone, groups are much safer." Disappointed, we turned to Turkey only to find that the weather was 50 degrees, at best, so we were back to the drawing board.

Looking again at South America, I noticed three small countries on the eastern hump: French Guinea, Surinam and Guyana. Back at the library, I investigated further and discovered that French Guinea was flat, undeveloped and sparsely populated. Surinam was more populated with some industry and more diverse terrain and Guyana was undeveloped, sparsely populated with mostly jungle and bush country. After checking with the airlines I found that Guyana was the only possibility because of flight availability and cost.

I looked at the maps and read more books. Fortunately, traveling in the jungle appealed to both of us even though road travel was neither mentioned nor shown on the maps. Rivers were everywhere! Until 1966, Guyana had been a British Colony. Since it had been British Guiana from 1814-1966, it seemed reasonable and unconscionable that the English had not used their technology to create bridges and roads to explore their empire. I figured that the maps or books I used were obsolete. Computers weren't very smart then, and many questions were still a puzzle as we flew through the clouds in a British West Indies airplane, knowing each moment we were closer to our answers.

It didn't seem long before we were landing in Port of Spain, Trinidad and transferring to a plane for Georgetown, the capital of Guyana. Waiting in line with us to reboard stood a small pleasant-looking woman. She smiled, as I did in return. I noticed she was holding a Guyanese passport. Starting a conversation, I asked her if there were roads into the interior. "No," she answered, "there is only one road in the country and that is along part of the coast. It stops and starts, so to follow the coast you have to take boats on or across the rivers, walk on paths or take a bush plane." She smiled again, chose her seat, and disappeared from view. Lee and I sat further back and watched in silence as we left the tarmac.

And so here we were in 1990, flying in a coal-black sky with lights twinkling on the wings when the pilot announced, "We will now make our descent into Georgetown. Please make sure your seat belts are fastened."

There were no city lights to show the existence of humans as our plane was descending ... no urban luminescence of any kind to show warmth and life. Approaching the landing strip, only a few lights illuminated the runway and airport. Everything else was dark and invisible. It was as if we had dropped through black nothingness with a few lights as our savior.

The plane's propellers stopped, the door was opened and we cautiously walked down the steps to begin our adventure. We followed the other passengers into a small cement block terminal to customs where we were directed to one of three lines: diplomats, citizens and non-residents. I saw two elderly white-haired gentlemen in the diplomat's line. Most people were in the citizen's line. Only a few of us remained in the third line.

A man from India stood with us. "Make sure you declare any jewelry and money you are bringing into the country. Fill in the documents correctly or the agents may confiscate any undeclared excess when you leave the country. I come here often on business and am very careful what I do and say." Then he added, "Be sure to exchange all dollars on the black market since the hotels or banks give one-half of what the black market gives. "But, be sure to exchange only 50 dollars at a time to keep the stack of bills manageable since you get 55 Guyanese dollars to one American dollar." Then he was called to customs.

I could feel many eyes upon us and looking around, I realized why. Everyone was dark, very dark, and I looked like a freckled albino with red hair from some alien country. I knew, from reading, that the largest ethnic group was the Indo-Guyanese. Their immigration started from the mid-1800s until 1917, when over 200,000 immigrants from East India landed in Guyana. It all began in the 1830s with the "Gladstone Experiment," a scheme of indentureship. They were promised passage over, indentureship for five years and passage back, but the plan was filled with fraud and deceit. As my mind was reviewing this, I heard a man calling us to customs.

"Why are you here?" the agent asked.

Lee said, "We are tourists." The customs area was small and our voices and surrounding voices responded a pitch lower and quieter. Since privacy seemed to be of concern, the tones came out a gravelly whisper.

The agent then asked, "How much money do you have?"

"$500 each," I replied.

He looked in disbelief at us standing there with only knapsacks the size of book bags and said, "And is that the only luggage you have?" We nodded. He took our passports to another man and they both stood talking, flipping the pages of our passports and looking over at us. Then our agent came back, stamped our passports with a loud smack and looked up. "There are taxis out front that you can take to town."

"How far is it to the city?" I asked.

"A forty-minute ride," he answered dismissively.

We walked out into the lobby. It was simply built with no frills of any sort. At this hour, there was no information booth, banking or food service available. We were hoping to see someone to latch on to and share a ride into the city, but no one was around. When we stepped outside, everyone had already disappeared, leaving us on our own.

Instantly, a myriad of bodies surrounded us pushing and shouting, "You want a cab, lady? You want a taxi, white man? Wanna exchange some American dollars? I give you a good deal." I felt like a morsel of food dropped in a fish tank for a school of starving fish.

As I looked over the pool of faces I saw a neatly dressed, small Indian in khaki shorts, look at us, shake his head and walk away. The men and boys surrounding us started tugging on our arms and fighting among themselves while saying, "We will take you to Georgetown. Here, here is the car."

Lee bravely said, "We want a minibus (since they were numbered and had 'taxi' written on them giving them legitimacy)."

Then a large man came motioning us towards his car. "Get in," he said, "I will take you to town for 15 American dollars, get in, get in." The young boys continued to wail at our sides chanting, "Exchange money, exchange money," while we stood immobile and confused.

All of a sudden the neatly dressed Indian I had noticed earlier walked up. "My name is Ronald and I have a taxi van. I will take you to Georgetown for 15 American dollars. Do you want to come?" Lee and I looked at one another and answered, "Yes!" Ronald then opened the door and we jumped in.

The other drivers were furious and said to our driver, "You will use a whole bus to take them? You are foolish."

Meanwhile, the young boys were thrusting their hands through the open windows yelling, "We give you 45 of our dollars for one American. Please, please!"

As Ronald drove away, we closed our windows on their eager faces. At the same time, we said, "Thank you!"

The vehicle was muggy with no air conditioning. Outside was black as black can be. I opened my window with a sigh of relief at having landed safely and also finding a ride that felt safe. We rode in silence a few moments before Ronald put a tape in his cassette. He drove down the dark road, the headlights from the car the only bright eyes. The roads were bumpy ... Ronald drove on the left side (it had been an English colony) and we rode with the calypso music wafting through the air. "Why is everything so quiet and dark, are we that far from civilization?" I asked.

"The country has very little fuel for their generators and allows the citizens only a few hours of electric in the late afternoon or early morning. The wealthy have their own generators, but most can't afford one."

The road wound endlessly. Ronald turned down the radio and asked. "Would you like to stop for a beer?"

"No," I answered. "We just want to find a hotel."

Once more we rode in silence. The darkness, as pervasive as a coal miner's tunnel, surrounded us until a house appeared along the road and jolted our senses, a reminder that we were on the ground rather than somewhere surreal.

The atmosphere felt more alive as the density of houses started to increase ... many were on stilts. I asked Ronald if the water level changed during the rainy season. "No, he said. "People build high off the ground so they can cook outdoors and still have protection during the rainy season. Wood or kerosene is used for cooking and with the odor or smoke, it's much more pleasant to cook outdoors. When it rains the children have a place to play. But if a person gains wealth then he closes the area in, showing that he can afford more finished space."

All of a sudden we were in Georgetown driving through an area of dilapidated warehouses. There were still no streetlights but every car honked in passing, like two souls passing with their eyes fixed and shining—wanting company in the darkness. I could see some people sitting against the buildings and some lying on the ground sleeping under the eaves of the buildings, trying to use all available protection from the elements. Then we came to a square with locals milling about. There were vendors with carts selling food and drinks. Cars and taxis sat idle. People of different sizes and shapes were aimlessly wandering about in the dark. I felt like I was at a stranger's house when the electricity went out, and losing most of my sight, had to rely on the host's directions.

Ronald drove up to a white stucco hotel. Lee and he went in while I waited. Lee came out and said, "It's $50 American. Let's try somewhere else." So we tried two other places. One was full and one was $65. We went back to the first place. It was midnight and we were exhausted. We had been up since 5 a.m. We exchanged some money with Ronald, paid him for the ride, and thanked him profusely for helping us.

"Do you have time tomorrow to be our guide and exchange more money?" I asked.

"I will be here at nine in the morning to answer any questions and help you find your way around. Goodnight," he said.

We were happy to have a place to sleep. Even though it was more money than we had wished to spend, we were grateful for the air conditioner: it was an escape and comfort from the heat, the mugginess of the night and the invasive silent darkness.

Getting ready for bed I noticed literature on the nightstand. And I read: "We welcome you to the Tower Hotel and wish you a very pleasant stay. We strongly advise that you follow these recommendations to assure that your visit is safe and enjoyable. Please keep your windows locked, your doors locked, and your valuables with you at all times. Please show your pass key to the guards for admittance to the hotel. Please do not stay out on the streets after 6 p.m. Please walk only on those streets where you see policemen or safety guards. Please read the enclosed evacuation instructions in case of a fire. We are happy you chose our hotel and hope to be of service to you on a return trip to Georgetown." Questions were drifting around in my mind but I was too exhausted to think anymore ... sleep came easy.

Our alarm went off at 8:30 a.m. and after quickly showering

in the available cold water, we hurriedly got ready and raced to the corner to meet Ronald for coffee. Lee and I were starved! We ordered four egg sandwiches and coffee. The sandwiches were small and dry; the coffee was thick and sweet, but it all tasted delicious. After we finished eating Ronald still hadn't arrived, so Lee ran down the block to a bakery to get some bread for later and I bought two more cups of thick coffee. Both men arrived at the same time.

Ronald greeted us, "How did you sleep?"

"Like logs," Lee replied. "We're rested and ready to go. I guess the first thing we need to do is get some money. Also, Judi was telling me about some secluded Amerindian village that sounds rather interesting. It's deep in the jungle? Do you know anything about it?"

"I know who to ask," Ronald replied. "They're not far from here and then we can go to my sister's pawn shop. She will be able to exchange your dollars at a good rate. You ready? My cousin needed the van today so we're on foot. Are your packs too heavy to carry for a while?"

"No. We're good," I replied.

It was already 80 degrees and muggy at only 10 a.m. It did feel oppressive, but we didn't feel the heat until we had raced after Ronald and come to a stop in front of a weathered clapboard building labeled, "Interior Government of Guyana."

Two paunchy men in uniform were sitting on chairs guarding the entrance. We stood quietly while Ronald talked to them. One of the men stood up and escorted us into the building, muttered something to a secretary and turned and said, "Wait, he'll be with you shortly." So we sat on the two available folding chairs and stared at either the sweating air conditioner protruding from the bellied moist wall and the water-stained picture of Mr. Official hanging askew next to it, or the heavy-set girl sitting behind the receptionist's desk. Since there were only two seats, Ronald offered them to us and stood looking into space.

My chair was next to the receptionist's desk. She was attempting to look busy; she walked to the file cabinet and took out a folder and kept flipping through the same pages scrutinizing them microscopically like she was looking for fly scat. I smiled to myself. This could be any bureaucratic office in the world.

Eventually, Lee and Ronald were called into the office. I stayed behind sitting in my folding chair. Soon I was called in, too.

There were two alternatives open to us: a private guide plus two government documents plus a three-week wait (not an option/ we had less than two weeks); or leaving in a few days with some ornithologists on a guided excursion since they had two vacancies and needed the money to keep their costs down. The group was going for one week into the jungle and staying at an Amerindian camp. From there they would take daily hikes out to observe birds. This sounded way too academic to us, plus it would keep us in Georgetown three more days to get things in order.

We thanked the gentleman, left the building and resumed our walk. We listened to Ronald and realized that since 80% of Guyanese lived outside of Georgetown, it made sense to go on our own to small villages. Going north sounded more interesting since there were fewer and smaller villages. This should give us a real feel for rural Guyana.

"Do they have any banks there?" I asked.

Ronald laughed. "I'm talking country. You best get the money you think you'll need from my sister."

"Do you think $200 will be enough for a week?"

"Sounds a lot to me," Ronald said, "but if that's what you want, my sister has it." To get to the shop, which Ronald said was in the heart of Georgetown, we had to walk down a boulevard. Walking down the boulevard I could feel the presence of the English. Large leafy trees lined the sidewalk. Their trunks were all painted white from the ground up to a six-foot level as if they were trying to simulate white pillars. The trees stood among small white stucco benches that lined the walkway. It had the appearance of a pristine park. Peering at us through the trees on our side of the street was an extremely well-kept hotel. I took Lee's hand and pulled him over to look at it. Ronald followed. It was so picturesque with its newly painted forest green eaves laden with baskets of greenery that masked an interior courtyard. Looking up at the eaves from the sidewalk teased my curiosity. "Do you think, Ronald, it would be okay to go in?"

He nodded. I asked a guard for permission to look at the hotel.

The guard took us up a staircase into the courtyard and to a room that was invisible from the street. The ceiling was very high, vaulted, and of polished mahogany ... the floor was a mirror image. All the floral urns and furniture were made of white wicker. All seat cushions were white ... crisp white uniforms adorned all the employees. Even the baby grand on the stage in the corner of the room was painted white!

I sat in one of the chairs and my mind flipped back the pages of time to the English regime. I could see women in pastel and white dresses carrying parasols with their male companions in khaki and white, wearing spectacles on their droll faces ... chatting, maybe laughing, socializing in their cocoon or picturesque pro-tected environment, ignoring the unsophistication outside their walls. As I was thinking how suffocated I would have felt living in their cloister, I was jolted from my thoughts, relieved to see the greenery hanging from the eaves. I remembered that we had to get back on the boulevard and find our way to the pawn shop.

We hurried outside to resume our walk and as we sauntered along, both the presence and the absence of the English could be felt; some benches needed painting and the boulevard was not as immaculate as it had appeared earlier. Ronald commented that these were difficult times for the Guyanese. "The English took their industries with them. The leadership following has been even more self-serving, leaving many impoverished and many others with little hope."

Finally, we arrived at the pawn shop. It was a white frame building on the corner with large overhead doors now open to the sidewalk and allowing the public to walk through. Guards in white uniforms stood watching the public and the showcases, their eyes restless and darting with scrutiny for the slightest change in activity. Behind the cases were two attractive and petite women, both on the phone; one of them nodded as we entered. While waiting, I looked in the cases. Gold and silver jewelry, silverware and artifacts looked up at me, traded by their owners for a few dollars ... there was an aroma of poverty in the air.

The woman who had nodded a greeting finished on the telephone and came over. Ronald introduced his sister Sandy and we gave her our two hundred American dollars. She advised that we go into an inconspicuous area of the shop since that was an inordinate amount of money to exchange at once. A severe recession was ongoing; only small bills were available. The Guyanese currency we received was two inches high! Lee had trousers with three pockets running down each leg. He proceeded to put some bills into each pocket and some into a sock pinned to his undershorts. I divided mine between my secret sock, purse and knapsack. Armed with monetary sustenance, we were now ready for the rural villages of Guyana.

Ronald encouraged us to move along since the heat would be getting worse later in the day and would make travel more uncomfortable. "I can feel it already," Lee said. My skin agreed in silence: It was sweating and sticky as I raced after Lee and Ronald. We walked through the older parts of Georgetown, arriving at the open market, the oldest section of the city, where the boats docked or sailed with their merchandise. The maze of stalls and "wandering" merchants was perched on the edge of the sea, the Caribbean Sea. Approaching the water I could see the scows, tugs and ships bobbing in the water like corks on fishing lines. And with the refuse of the merchants and fisherman floating on the water, it gave the frontage an appearance of a swamp ... the debris causing the waves to look sluggish and almost animated, as with each lap they heaved a sigh of relief when some litter was pushed onto land.

The cries of the merchants distracted me. The stalls were tiny and compact and as we continued our walk; many smiled at us while others tried their sales plea. The most picturesque were the men and women selling items off of trays hanging from their necks, or long necklaces of food products. As they chanted a song about their wares, their bodies moved and swayed. A man with small bags of sugar attached to one another in a chain around his neck stopped me in my tracks. His singing and animation had magic that was as reminiscent and as luring as the Pied Piper of Hamelin.

CHAPTER TWO

Bartica

A s Ronald guided us to the buses he gave us his final pointers. "Since there is only one road along the coast, you will not get lost. Sometimes there will be a river to cross that is running into the sea. Then you must take a boat to continue. In rainy season many parts of the roads are impassable. You should have no trouble this time of the year."

He found our bus (a VW van since nothing larger could manage the roads), wished us well, and disappeared into the crowd. When we got in, the van already felt full with eight people, but by the time we left there were 20 people young and old with bags, bundles and umbrellas filling every inch of space. The unresolved mystery was how the door could slide open and let someone off or on without spilling passengers onto the road.

As we were driving away, the heat of the day was arriving. It was a blazing 95 degrees accompanied by mugginess. The merchants were drooping and the shoppers were leaving. A sea of umbrellas popped up as everyone covered themselves and scurried for shelter. I watched the locals fleeing the heat as I sat sweating, wedged between two women fanning themselves with their hankies, swearing under my breath that I hadn't noticed that the window by my seat was permanently closed.

Lee didn't look much more comfortable. He was sitting on a small fold-down seat by the door. With every stop, he had to either get out or be squished aside. Finally, we drove out of Georgetown and the chaos and heat seemed to subside. Most riders were talking to one another and although I could understand the gist of their conversation, they spoke rapidly and with an unusual English dialect leaving me with observation as the only option. (English was the language of Guyana, but as we were to learn, there were different dialects because of the Indian, Amerindian and African influences.)

School was getting out when we drove through our first small village. The children came out running and yelling. They all wore uniforms that were color-coordinated by age. The youngest wore orange shorts or jumpers, the middle group wore green and the oldest children wore brown. As they pushed each other around, they seemed oblivious to the heat of the day or the animals grazing or resting in their pathway. The pigs, goats and cows seemed equally uninterested in the children and continued to commune with nature or make their animal sounds; at times they would look into space as though truly thinking, simultaneously wiggling or switching their tails and then solemnly retracing their steps as though they just remembered something.

As we drove along the coast, the little villages were mirror images of one another. Their schoolyards were grass-barren; their school buildings were windowless with shutters, built up on stilts to have a protected play area during the rainy season. And there were always a few Guyanese walking down the road. I felt the momentum of the people; someone was walking, someone was getting out of the bus or into the bus. Only the bodies in the bus changed as the bus rolled down the road like an overstuffed sausage at its bursting capacity.

At times we could see the endless blue of the ocean and at times we drove deeper inland. But anytime we saw irrigation ditches coming from the ocean, there was dairy or crop farming. The homes were neat and simple, but I didn't see any indication of available lodging. Where would we stay?

Soon the road stopped right on the bank of a large river. We had arrived at the small village of Parika. Lee and I unfolded out of the bus like tight springs popping out of a small box. Inhaling air into our lungs, we stood on a carpet of coconut shells and fruit peelings, mesmerized by the scene. The fish smell was so strong we could taste it and the merchants were singing out their calls of intrigue, while in the background small boys were recruiting riders for the water taxis, tugging at people's arms and pulling them towards the boats while we stood transfixed. Then we rose to the occasion and raced after our bus driver to ask if there were a place to stay. He smiled and said, "Hop in. I'll take you to the one place in town."

In a few minutes, we were there. It was someone's home and looked like all the other homes in the area … on stilts with the open-air living below and the house on top. When we drove up the entire family of five piled out to greet us. The three small children stood grinning and clinging to each other while their father took us up to see the house. It was one large room with two bedrooms divided off by long pieces of fabric hanging from the rafters. We would have one bedroom and the family the other. The remaining part of the floor space was the living area. Even though we were seasoned campers, we realized that we were used to more privacy. Since it was late afternoon there were enough hours left in the day that in such a "tight" living situation the day would feel endless. We asked our driver how close the next village was and if they had more hotels.

"I will take you to the pier. You can catch a boat to Bartica. There," he said, "you can find many hotels." Translating "many" as more than one, we agreed to gamble and went back to the waterfront.

Immediately, we were surrounded by young boys trying to sell us a seat on their friend's or family's water taxi. Lee and I were dying of thirst from our dusty morning ride so first we inhaled a drink at one of the stands and then followed our fearless young leaders to the taxi of their choice. We walked across the sand and onto the pier, which was joined by planks to a maze of extensions making some sections longer and some wider, probably to accommodate the seasonal change in depth of the water. Following the boys down the planks, we finally climbed down a ladder where the underside of the pier was visible. Here the taxis were tied to the piles and the underlying support structure was used as a catwalk to get to and from the boats. I walked down a two-by-four and jumped into the boat. There were only two remaining seats left in the bow. Luck was with us. We should be leaving shortly.

While we were waiting for the boat to leave Lee nudged me, "Look at the sky. A storm is moving in."

I looked up. "I can feel the wind, but maybe it will blow right by us." Just then the driver jumped in and started the motor, a new red Johnson 150 HP motor, which looked ludicrous on our small well-worn, low-riding wooden boat. The contrast made me smile.

Counting the passengers, I realized that maybe we needed the larger motor. Somehow 16 adults had squeezed into the space. Maybe the expense of the motor necessitated packing the boat with people and accounted for the fact that no life preservers were present because that space could be used for the profits from the fare for extra people and packages. The passengers seemed relaxed. I wanted to ask them if they knew that adult life jackets existed and if they felt anxious every time they relinquished their fate to their navigator and the river.

With the large motor sputtering because the propeller was not totally submerged into the water, the boys who had recruited us for the boat jumped into the water and pushed until the river was deep enough. I noticed the community of boats we were leaving behind. Did their shapes and colors reflect the personality and wealth of the owners? Some were bright, large, deep, and wide; some had motors, oars or sails. Many were dugouts sculpted from one tree. This intimated closeness with nature and appealed to me. But we were not Guyanese, we were visitors on our way to Bartica. Our navigator assured us there was plenty of lodging there because from Bartica men headed off into the jungle to mine diamonds or gold. "The Essequibo River is large and has much water that carries gold. Some of the miners live in Bartica, but many come from other villages," he said.

When our boat was safely away from any traffic, the driver opened the throttle and we flew down the river; the bow where we sat was suspended high above the water. A young boy was wedged in alongside me and as I laughed into the wind ... he joined in. The river was very wide, the water murky, and the banks were a wall of lush green foliage with breezes flirting with the leaves, their velvety appearance wafting and pulsating adventure across the water. My spirits were renewed with freshness and a zest for the moment. I felt transported into another time—if Tarzan had paddled by in a dugout or called from a tree on shore, I would have thought nothing of it.

I breathed deeply and threw my head back in delight. My hat

flew merrily away and my eyes saw the sky. It was still dark, or was it darker? I turned to Lee. "This should be interesting," he said as his head motioned to the sky. The wind seemed stronger even though it felt warm and good. The dark, robust clouds were persuading the sky to change its mood. We were only one-half hour into our two-hour journey, making the rain inevitable. Wedged in the boat like sardines in a tin made me feel very vulnerable, not afraid, but uncertain how the navigator would handle a storm. It was noisy, making it impossible for Lee or me to ask anyone around us. The other passengers lived with these weather changes all the time.

Noticing huts on stilts along the river in pairs, or sometimes alone, I wondered what it would be like to live this simply. Sometimes we passed a tiny island with only one or two huts looking out from a little spot of land. Surely they must have to move during the rainy season. Where did they go?

The waves were getting rougher. Lee and I were learning our first lesson in boat taxis: "Do not sit in the bow." The wooden seat smacked our behinds to remind us of our ignorance. Then the driver opened the throttle wide to try and beat the rain. I started to sit on my hands or push my feet against the roll of tarp on the floor to suspend myself above the seat, but I was still getting sore! Yet, despite everyone's wishes the winds got stronger and the rains moved in and it started to sprinkle.

Then the boat slowed down. Were we out of gas? I couldn't believe we weren't prepared. But the boat was just slowing down and headed toward two thatched huts on the shore. Soon the driver turned off the motor and pulled the propeller up out of the water while another man rowed closer to shore. Then a man and woman got out of the boat into the water. I was reminded of the obvious; this was a taxi and could drop people off at any time.

The woman held her skirt up above her knees as she climbed out of the boat. Her companion rolled his pant legs up, but not high enough. When he stepped into the river, the water seeped up his pant legs like oil on a wick. The couple called out "Thank you" as they balanced their purchased goods on their heads and steadied them with their hands. As we started up the motor once again they were both talking and laughing as they slowly walked towards shore … I wondered if this couple enjoyed their solitude.

My thinking was interrupted by a deluge from nature. The navigator shouted for us to unroll the tarp our feet rested on. All passengers pulled the oilcloth tarp onto their laps; it was even large enough to pull up over our heads. The driver, thinking he had given us sufficient protection, threw open the throttle and charged into the storm at a furious frantic speed. The impact of the boat against the waves shocked our insides and the torrential rain felt like gravel shot from a cannon, but I still could not hide my face under the tarp. Somehow it seemed incongruous that I should travel partway around the world and go undercover. It also seemed unbelievable that I was on a jungle river in a torrid rain in Guyana. I felt compelled to look through the veil of water pouring down the front of my face and bouncing on the waves of the river. I watched the greenery glisten and dance with the rain. The thatched huts, barely discernible, looked like small fortresses standing proud against the elements as we moved down the river in the storm. Maybe it was good to be in the bow of the boat so I could look out. The passengers in front of us had no interest in the rain and let the water run down the tarps and back into the river. I figured they had been through this many times before, or with the deluge and no life jackets they would be worried. It felt like the rains lasted forever (at least that's what my sore face felt). I was relieved when it changed from torrential to a steady rain and my butt wasn't smacked every second.

* * *

THE DRIVER WAS SLOWING down again. I wondered who was getting off this time. As the shoreline became visible so did the pier where a few people stood waving. Lee looked over at the boy wedged in next to me. "Is this Bartica?" he asked.

The boy nodded, "Yes," as he stood to wave and whistle at someone onshore.

Lee and I were the last to leave the boat. With my wet hair and clothes, I looked like I had fallen overboard. Lee had kept his hat on and tarp wrapped correctly so he looked as handsome as ever. The sky was just spitting lightly and the trees and rooftops were dripping from their overladen surfaces as we walked away from the dock. The residents stood around talking under the eaves of the buildings or walking as though the mist was nonexistent. Lee turned to me, a smile covering his face. "Now this is rural Guyana. That might be a road to the left of us but anything else in sight is a path. I don't know if a jeep could handle this terrain. Do you see a vehicle?"

I laughed. "I guess the books were right and I was wrong ... so much for my theory of 'there had to be roads.'"

"Let's start exploring our turf," Lee replied putting his arm around my shoulder and squeezing it.

As we were walking around the village the sun came back out. With all the rain the earth steamed, making us feel like we were in a big sauna. Bartica was a hilly village and soon our light packs became heavy, our backs wet, and our walk became a "trudge." We investigated four different hotels and were surprised to find that they were all filled. One clerk icily asked how we dare come without reservations!

We felt confused ... stunned at their aloofness. What had Lee and I done? Our appearances were neat and our behavior was not offensive. We went and sat by a table at Bing's, a snack shop open to the street, and had a beer. We needed to figure out what to do next. A young man walked up to us and asked, "Are you missionaries?"

After Lee replied, "No," he seemed very relieved and related that only locals and miners usually came to their village, the only others had been missionaries. The Barticans were suspicious of strangers, especially missionaries. Different religious groups had come and started churches, tried to change their thinking with medicine and supplies and then left.

We apologized for their behavior and repeated that we were just visiting and needed his help because we had tried to find lodging for the night and had been told that there were no rooms: "not for tonight or the next week." Our new acquaintance laughed and said, "We are funny people. Some have called us arrogant, but we are just proud; proud we have our independence and are surviving. Go back to one of the hotels and ask for a room but be very very patient. And tell them you are not missionaries. That will help."

We returned to the only hotel that had sofas in the lobby so we would have a place to "be patient" and inquired again about a room. It was on the second floor over a restaurant, which was not an asset, but we were attracted to the large balcony across the front of it. The clerk told us that the manager had gone home for dinner and would return in one or two hours.

"We came from Georgetown to visit your village. May we sit and wait?" I asked. "We are not missionaries but are traveling down the coast to explore your country." She nodded towards the sofas and mumbled something under her breath. I smiled in return and replied, "Thank you." For two hours we sat in a dimly lit lobby and waited until the manager returned and we were finally assigned a room, a room in an almost unoccupied hotel that cost four American dollars.

"Well," Lee whispered when we were given the key, "I wonder how long we would've waited if we'd told them we were missionaries." I burst out laughing.

Unlocking the door, we were surprised to find it was self-contained (toilet and shower) and had a mosquito net over the bed. "Guess what Lee," I said, after using the bathroom. "There's no hot water, but at least we have water."

Unpacking his backpack he turned to me, "I knew this was a classy place. I walked out on the balcony and noticed a pipe running down the outside of the building and into the river." (Our toilet also had running water but we never inquired about the location of the sewage plant.)

"Let's go find some food. We can come back and spend the evening on our balcony."

Our hotel proved to be an excellent location. It had a balcony off the second floor by our room. From there we could watch the schoolyard across the street, look to the left to see the main street, or to the right to see the river and rural landscape. Next door to the hotel was a small house on stilts with a lot of chickens in the yard and a goat and cow chewing any available grass. They were untethered, so if the grass looked the wrong shade of green or if they wanted to go visiting down the road, they just walked away (later that evening we saw the neighbor children run out to look for their grazing-family). The serious disadvantage was that below the hotel rooms was a restaurant and bar which contained a cement dance floor and two large speakers to entertain the local

Barticans and the departing miners. Unfortunately, the decibel level could probably reach those living in the bush within a five-mile radius. Their disco closed at 2 a.m.; then the roosters in the area "crowed" the final curfew ... and man, bird, and beast rested until the roosters lifted their voices again at sunrise. I never knew until Bartica that roosters could crow in the middle of the night.

However, the hotel was basically comfortable. Since it never gets cool, there were only louvered windows and the walls did not extend to the ceiling: this enabled the air to move around. Because we were near the bush with the malaria-bearing mosquito, the bed had a mosquito net hanging over it which hooked over the edges of the mattress with elastic. It was impossible to get out of bed without the entire net popping off the mattress so we had to negotiate any late-night bathroom visits.

While eating was not our priority, it was a necessity. Lucky for us, our demands were minimal but so were our options. We discovered our meals had to be purchased at the restaurant below or Bings a block away, where we could buy a potato or egg, dipped in batter and deep-fried, and wash it down with one of the available drinks: coffee, pop or beer. The place also served as the town library, where a local could rent a book for a few cents. Since Bings only had two tables to serve customers, we felt comfortable staying if the other table was empty. Other than snacks, any other food or groceries had to be purchased from open stalls or open markets.

In Bartica, there were only a handful of stores: a dry goods store, hardware and feed store, a grocery store with canned goods, and a dilapidated building called the police station, where movies were shown a few days a week. All other times the policeman sat in the doorway.

Since Bartica was nestled at the foot of hills populated with little houses and well-tread paths, we spent our days walking in the village and up into the hills. We snacked at Bings and chose any meals from the three items at the hotel. Their menu was the same for breakfast, lunch or dinner. Their diet was lean and consisted of mostly rice and chicken with no salad, bread or vegetables. Lee and I bought fresh fruit, canned fruit juice, and pop at the market to get enough fluids in our system. We could not drink the water and bottled water was hard to find. Our three staples at the hotel were "cook up" (which was rice cooked in coconut oil and generic meat bits thrown in), wild hog with brown sauce on rice and chicken stew.

Every meal we ate at the hotel was observed by maybe twenty people. However, they were not there to watch us, but to watch the only TV in the village—which just so happened to be in the restaurant. We had obviously chosen the "hottest" spot in the village and joined in the festivity ... only we chose to observe the native Barticans' faces as they watched the one and only channel. Understanding American English is quite difficult for the locals because their dialect was a sing-songy English Caribbean. The station came out of Miami via a huge satellite dish set up outside of the back of the hotel. The most interesting program was a Western with John Wayne which really got the audience going. The action in the story, obvious and simple, gave the audience complete comprehension. Their cathartic responses demonstrated the universal roller coaster of human emotion. Most of the time when advertisements came on they would laugh; they were seemingly treated as a cartoon since the rural Barticans could hardly relate.

After any meal, we took a walk and stopped in the most inconspicuous place we could find to watch the people. With little transportation in the village, the Barticans were noticeably muscular and thin. We saw only one overweight person. Walking was the means of transportation because of the daily rains and rutted roads and paths. Very few bicycles were used. During our stay, we saw two jeeps. The vehicles had maybe one mile of available dirt road upon which to drive and were owned by the two wealthiest families flaunting their assets, which incidentally also included hiring a barge to transport their jeeps down the river.

In the afternoon, the shops and stalls closed for a few hours. During that time the heat seemed unbearable, then the skies would turn from gray to black and the rains would fall torrentially for half an hour. Al, the owner of Bings called it a "sprinkle." "In the rainy season, it's nonstop for weeks," he added. I found this unfathomable. We were glad for Al. He was the only person in the village who socialized with us. The other locals never really conversed with us. They just answered our questions and moved on. Meanwhile, the Barticans put up their umbrellas and stood to chat in the deluge while we ran back to the hotel. Changing our clothes, we took ourselves to the balcony of the hotel and looking down the street watched the clusters of umbrellas. One afternoon we saw a man in a plastic raincoat. He looked hilarious and I'm sure he felt like he was in a steam bath with the 90-100 degree temperature.

The heat slowed everyone down but the children. Immobilized by the heat and temperature, we sat in shorts and loose shirts with bath towels under our buttocks, bed pillows behind our backs and our naked feet propped up on the balcony's ledge, hoping we didn't look too ridiculous but not caring. We watched the children at recess in the school yard across the street. They were having relays as we were sitting there panting! A vendor, with his donkey pulling a small cart of bananas, stood nearby at the beck and call of the children. Intermittently a child would run up with a few coins, grab a banana, peel and toss the skin onto the ground, devour the banana and then quickly get back into action. At that point, our goat from next door would perform the function of a vacuum by running up and inhaling the peeling! So the grounds were kept immaculate. Lee turned to me. "Would you call this the Bartican ecosystem?" I smiled in response.

"Remember the kids we saw in Amizmiz last year? He added. "That was a great trip!"

I laughed. "I think the highlight was those baby goats. But we sure lucked out hooking into that flight!" Somehow, I had been surfing the computer and found a ridiculously inexpensive fare to Marrakesh, Morocco, for ten days including lodging. I do believe they thought I was a travel agent. Nevertheless, we went and loved it. Lee was a natural, guiding us around the souks. We visited many small shops and stalls. One day a young man, who wanted us to be his sponsor and come to America, followed us for hours. The kneeling of men in the square at the call to the mosques was unforgettable to witness.

"I don't remember the couple we took the side trip with to Amizmiz," Lee said, "but I'll never forget the market and that smiling man in his turban and coat of many colors with a cloth bag hanging on his arm with two white furry-headed kids hanging their heads out."

"Me either. I'm glad we got a photo. I remember that velvety green grass blanketing the hills was even lusher than a putting green on the golf course. Hard to explain, isn't it?"

And we turned back to watch a goat eat a banana peel.

* * *

ONE MORNING WE CHOSE to walk further away from Bartica along the river bank. After passing a very dejected and dilapidated building labeled, "The Hospital," we came upon a very well-manicured park with a beach, bleachers and a little gate house maybe 12 by 15 feet. As we walked into the park, a small woman came out of the house to greet us, "Hello, may I help you?"

Lee explained we were tourists exploring Bartica and just stumbled upon the park on one of our walks.

"My name is Monica," she said. "Let me show you around. Did you walk by our hospital on the way?" she asked. "Years past it was a place where we would go to get medicine and receive help, but today it is where people go to die who have no hope or no families. There is very little medicine available in Guyana and now we have no help from the church that left us a few years ago and went back to the states. My country doesn't have money for medicine, so we rely on many of our old remedies."

With that, she changed the subject and started to tell us about the park. Smiling she said, "The bleachers are for the races we have two times in the summer. The men who drive the water taxis and their friends all race against each other and it is very festive. Since the river is right here and the park is so nice, I must stay here all the time to make sure that people from the country or up the river do not come and make tents and live here forever." Monica pointed to some people in the river washing clothes. "If I do not watch these people they will hang their clothes on the fence and be here all day; I allow them to wash but not to linger." We walked over to the bleachers and watched the locals in the river.

The women were socializing while washing and beating their clothes. I was getting hot, and they must have felt it too. As a finale to all their hard labor, the women swam out to neck level, took off their clothes, washed them with a bar of soap, put them back on and casually walked out of the water to go on their way.

Just then we saw a boat with eight men go by loaded down with gear. "My husband is off in the bush," Monica said. "Maybe the men in that boat will be joining him at the same mine." We all waved as they went by. "Most men of Bartica make their living this way. They set up mines deep in the bush and move on until they no longer find any gold. Equipment cannot be taken into such simple surroundings. Men are used instead. The lead man goes under water with a suction hose in hand to send the sludge up to his mates. On his face is a mask giving him air. He can only stand the work for a few hours at a time, alternating with another diver until their 12-hour shift is up. The men "on top" are continuously washing the sludge in a big box that has a screen at the bottom. With time all the sand and mud is washed away leaving either pebbles or gold."

Sounds brutal, I thought to myself.

Monica said that most men kept going to the mines until they were physically unable to do the job ... it reflected being a man. It was adventurous and the pay was good. Their share of the profits could support the family for three to six months. During the rainy season, the miners stayed home for two months; otherwise, they came home, intermittently for a few weeks, getting restless very quickly.

"There are many parties during the heavy rains," she said. "Everyone is happy that the men are home. But when the sun starts to shine, off they go again and things are back to their old self."

We learned that in the village most jobs were held by women. They were the main moral and monetary support for their families. However, since the men were forced to retire from mining during middle age, there were men in the village who worked, too. Maybe their physical endurance was no longer great enough to remain in the bush for months on end. Nevertheless, most of the men still had enough stamina to play on a soccer team in the village.

We sat and watched the soccer game from our chairs on the hotel balcony. Almost daily there was a game across the street in the school yard. It was held mid-day after classes were out and the heat had subsided. But that did not mean that there were no rains to contend with! Down came the rains and up came the umbrellas of those standing and watching. The players pretended there was no rain, dancing around the puddles, falling and getting up as though they were part of a gymnastics team. If a man fell into a puddle, the fans howled in delight as he shook himself off like a wet puppy dog and kept playing in the game. Nature and the Bartican natives had learned to live together.

* * *

OUR STAY WAS ENJOYABLE but it was time to explore another village in Guyana. One day as we were buying some juice and talking to Al at Bing's, we asked about villages further up the coast. He had a topographical map of the area to keep track of his mining friends. Laying the map on our table, he talked as he showed us the surrounding area. "Go back up the river and cross to the other side. There is a road along the coast. Take this road to its end. There you will find a very small place called Charity. It is the last village north before endless jungle and bush. The Amerindians and miners must come to this village for buying and trading their produce or gold. There are two places to stay and since you will be there before the weekend they should both have rooms. Charity comes to life on Friday. Everyone comes on the river to sell, buy, trade, chat and drink rum. It is like a big party for one day and then the people go back home and all is very quiet. It is a nice place."

The decision was unanimous, the opportunity irresistible. It sounded like the edge of the earth.

"Oh," he then added, "instead of eating at your hotel tonight, try something different. If you walk down the street and take the first left, you'll see a white house with stairs on the outside to the second floor. Walk up and taste my friend Gloria's lo mein. Tell her I sent you."

Eager for a change on the menu, we followed Al's instructions and went to look for Gloria. We walked in and didn't feel unwelcome. I guess the news had spread that we weren't missionaries. There were just a few tables and one was vacant. There were only two menu choices; I got the lo mein, and Lee got the chow mein. He was the lucky one: I got food poisoning. Later that evening, I was upchucking and miserable. Lee said, "Let's wait another day."

"No," I replied. "We won't get a room if we don't get there before the weekend."

We checked out of the hotel at six the next morning. My stomach was empty and still somewhat queasy. I must've looked it. A young boy approached us, "Follow me," he said and took us to the boat where he insisted we sit near the driver. "Best seat," he added. Some Barticans waved as the boat left the harbor. I doubt it was at us but maybe it was ... the topic of gossip would no longer be available.

CHAPTER THREE

Charity

The boat moved out of the Barticans' view and sped up the river. The water was smooth as glass and without turbulence, my tummy already felt better. We sped effortlessly along; the sun was still sleeping under the clouds and the warm early morning air moved gracefully around us. It was delightful. We passed children picking each other up in their dugouts and then passed the school where all their boats were lined up and the students were playing before their school day began. I realized that all peaceful childhoods had a common thread ... they shared the same laughter in the playground and eagerness for the day.

Our navigator maneuvered up the river. It didn't seem long before he was tilting the motor out of the water and securing the boat, and Lee and I were standing on a pier in Parika. A few young boys, recognizing us from before came running over, "Hello, hello friends, where do you go? We know a good driver." They guided us to a boat that would be going across the river to Supenaam. As we sat waiting, I noticed that at the end of the dock sat a little house with a trough extending from its underside out over the water. Standing by the house was an old woman holding a rope attached to the handle of a bucket. She pushed the bucket off the dock into the water. After the bucket had filled with water the woman pulled it up, set it on the dock and waited until someone walked in to use the facility and came back out. Then she opened the door, took her bucket of water and washed any remaining evidence into the river. The river moved so fast that any excrement would quickly be lost at sea.

Our boat was now packed and we were ready to leave. It was mid-morning and already steamy hot. I covered up as much as I could; in addition, Lee coated every visible inch of my fair body with double-digit sunscreen. The other people were looking at my jacket, hat with a scarf over it and tied under my chin, and dark glasses. Lee laughed and whispered, "Good thing I love you, even though you do look like a missionary!"

"You're just lucky you can take the heat with your Heinz 57 complexion. I'm a sweet Swede with fair skin and I have to watch it." The heat was quite unbearable, and I didn't feel like broiling my skin. After riding across the water for 45 minutes with the sun's rays bouncing off the water onto my face, I was glad I had taken precautions.

We arrived at our destination, "Supenaam," and climbed out of the boat onto the dock. It was a speck of a place with two stands selling homemade food and one vacated and very worn building with an attached peeling sign which read, "Malaria Kills. Please notify your health service if you have chills and fever." I had the feeling that the building had once been the health service. Planning our trip I had called the Guyanese embassy to ask about vaccinations. They had said, "You don't need any." I had also called the infectious disease clinic at Cleveland Clinic and they told me that we should have typhoid and cholera shots, also quinine tablets for malaria, but that nothing was available ... the military in the Gulf

War had taken their supply.

I had put this out of my mind until now. Lee and I looked at one another in dismay. "We'll have to risk it. I have an American Express card in the sock safety pinned to my underpants. Hopefully, there's enough credit to fly us home in an emergency."

Lee laughed.

A few cars and people were loitering. Lee found us a taxi. The driver had a thick accent; we confirmed our destination, "Charity," with the other couple in the car. They nodded in assent. We sat in the front seat with the sizzling sun reflecting off the dashboard of the car. The pink fake-fur-covered dash featured Indian statues glued upright onto the fur. I felt like I was looking at a shrine in the backyard of a doll house. I asked about the decoration.

"My wife and daughter do this for me," the driver answered with a big smile.

We looked out at the scenery for maybe 20-30 minutes and then the road got busier. It was the town of Suddie. A few minutes later we passed a big building.

"That is our hospital. It is a place where you go to die" (repeating the exact words that Monica had told us a few days earlier). He continued to drive, and then later, turning inland he added, "I must stop at the market for wife. Watch for me to leave. We go again very soon," and after parking the car, he jumped out to run his errand.

"Let's grab something to drink," Lee said. We purchased two bottles of orange pop from a nearby vendor and then we wandered around the market for a few minutes perusing stands within the view of the car. Our interest was getting to Charity and not missing our ride. It was not long before the driver came back to his car and opened the trunk to load his packages, and opened the doors for two new riders who had magically appeared.

* * *

THE COUNTRYSIDE WAS BEAUTIFUL, with lush fields containing grazing cattle, and cultivated and growing crops. How did they get their produce to market? We drove by peas or beans drying on a tarp positioned in the sun on the road. A few rocks or logs held down the edges of the tarp. There were already huge pot holes in the road creating a real obstacle course for the driver. Another couple stood awaiting a ride; people got in and out but the car was never full and remained amazingly quiet. (We were probably the reason for their discomfort.) I felt like asking questions and Lee, being the quieter one, did not venture to ask any. One time I broke the silence to ask how far. "Soon," the driver said. Traveling down the road I could see we were approaching a large blue truck with a canopied chassis on the back. A group of people was standing around the truck. What had happened? Coming closer I could see a man weighing out beans on a scale for a customer. It was a grocery store on wheels!

We kept on driving for two hours. Every settlement we passed through made me wonder, "Is the next place Charity?" Finally, we came to the end of the road and the Pomeroon River. An Indian was pushing sugar cane through a wringer and throwing the squeezed stalks into the water. Men were waiting for a drink of cane juice from the tub. There were a few other stalls and a few other people. Our driver in his sing-songy English asked the four of us for $2 each for the ride to Charity. With the cost of petroleum at $2.50 per gallon, and the road conditions so bad, how could he afford to eat?

We got out and looked around. There was no town; just the sugar cane merchant and three stands under the pavilion on the water's edge ... the edge of the earth. Lee bent to whisper in my ear. "Folks are looking at us. This is an outpost before there is 'nowhere.'"

"I'm sure they're wondering why we're here," I replied. One man echoed my words, asking if we were missionaries, since that was the only other white people he had seen. Smiling, we informed him that we were two Americans who just wanted to visit his village.

Lee and I started walking back down the road toward the sign we could see on a building, "Xenon." It was the name that the merchant in Bartica had given us to stay. A few people walked with us, welcoming us to their village and assuring us that the Xenon was a fine place to stay. We walked across some planks, over a ditch and entered. The landlord greeted us and immediately offered us a room that was similar to the one we had left that morning. We felt at home with our mosquito net, our balcony off the front, and the restaurant and disco below, and were elated to see there wasn't any satellite dish or TV.

A very petite Amerindian woman, descendants of the Mayans, came up and introduced herself. She said her name was Pauleen and wanted to know ours. She also informed us that if we needed something to eat we had to order in advance since people mainly came to drink and play pool. Both Lee and I were hungry and welcomed anything Pauleen could come up with. Our English was mutually difficult to understand but we understood she would come to get us when something was ready. An hour later we were in the bar eating a bowl of meat cubes with a spicy sauce on it (which we later found out was deer) and using a thin flour pancake with dried white peas sticking to it, called dhal puri to wrap the meat in. It was delicious!

Lee and I returned to our room. We spent the evening sitting on chairs, in the shadows cast from the balcony wall, on the roof overhanging the entrance of the building. In silence we watched the men walk down the road and come into the bar to socialize. Sometimes they brought their families with them. To enter the Xenon they had to cross a small foot bridge over a trench bringing water from the river. Sometimes a man would walk out onto the bridge and urinate into the water. (I felt embarrassed to be a spectator.)

The evening was still. The moonlight was the villagers' lantern. Lee and I were sitting in a trance when we heard footsteps behind us. "Hello," a voice said. "My name is Phillip. I tend bar downstairs but will come up to chat with you when I get a chance."

"Great to meet you," Lee said, as we both stood to see who our intruder was.

"It is peaceful," he added. "There is electric, but the people can't afford the gasoline for their generators, or to buy a generator for that matter. The Xenon can afford both a generator and gasoline and by its luminescence draws people in. We'll talk soon. I was curious to meet the new hotel guests." He smiled, then turned around and left.

Lee and I returned to our chairs and watched the folks walk down the road to homes where food was cooked by kerosene or wood fires. We could smell the wood smoke and spice from the cooking. When darkness came, we were still sitting on our balcony watching shadows on a moon-lit night. And we watched the moonbeams reflect off of the small waves in the trench as they quietly moved along the road toward the mother-water.

* * *

THE RIVER DREW US like a magnet. Each day we spent exploring the river bank, walking along any path that we could follow. One day we came to a very simply constructed gate in our pathway.

Thinking it was to keep cows from straying; we moved the structure and kept walking. The greenery became denser and the trees
seemed of gargantuan height.

I threw my hands into the air and shouted, "I feel like Alice in
Wonderland." Lee smiled and bent to kiss my forehead. "You love
this, don't you?" he said. As I looked up at the trees so animated
and humongous, I felt like a tiny miniature creature. Giant palms
stood very tall waving their arms of fanned leaves over my head.
The pineapple trees stood proudly at their side, their huge fruits
camouflaged by color except for a subtle purple flower that stood
out as a marker. Mixed in, were coconut trees at various stages of
growth, their varying sizes and shapes adding to the mysterious
feel of the interior. The sun peered down through the openings

in the trees, making some green leaves very rich and others very transparent. Nature was all around, making me assess my insignificance in the scheme of things. The feeling precipitated was not fear but tranquility from seeing a crystal clear picture ... Lee and I held hands and kept walking.

We noticed the sun beams were disappearing and that dusk was upon us so we retraced our steps down the path. As we returned to the gate, a little Indian woman came running toward us. She was followed by three children in thread-bare clothing. Behind them was a clearing with a very weathered small structure that I assumed was their dwelling. She smiled as she approached and said, "Welcome to our home."

We were totally embarrassed for trespassing on her property and Lee apologized before adding, "It was one of the most spectacular places we have ever seen."

She asked where we were from and was thrilled to talk about their trees and land and offered us a drink of coconut milk. Her oldest daughter ran to get a long pole leaning against the house and then swung at a coconut until she hit one down. The girl was small but knew how to handle a machete and taking the knife cut a hole in the end and drained the milk into glasses that one of the smaller children had retrieved. Handing us each a glass she said, "Drink."

We both lifted our glasses. It tasted oily and warm. Looking into the glass I noticed a viscous substance that had settled at the bottom. The woman said, "You must drink the meat too. It is the best part." Feeling like an honored guest or initiate of a secret society, I knew I must drink it all. Holding my breath I tipped the white slimy stuff down my gullet. "What a treat," I said.

Just then an old man came walking toward us. I have never

seen such an ancient-looking human. His clothes had been patched so many times the original material was hardly discernible. His shoes were tied on with strings. He stopped where we were and smiled a toothless smile, and I noticed that he was terribly thin. His pants were held up by a rope that also held his machete. On his shoulder was slung a burlap sack.

His wife was chatting while introducing us to her husband, telling us that the sack contained coffee beans that he had been harvesting all day. He opened the sack and held the beans in his hands, gnarled hands that had worked a million hours. The beans looked like cranberries which had to be peeled and dried before they were ready for use.

He told us about their farm. They had 10 children, six of them boys, but none had remained with the work so hard. It was subsistence for the family now since they could only harvest what they themselves could do. They could not find local laborers to work for a reasonable wage. There would be no money left for their family if they paid very high wages to harvest plus paid shipping to Georgetown. The farm used to be prosperous and now they could barely eek a living by selling any extra that they had at the market in Charity. The husband went to the house and came back with oranges and grapefruit for us to take. He wanted us to sample all of his good fruits.

Feeling such intimacy in their sharing, neither of us knew what to do. We did not want to insult their sense of pride by offering the shirts off our backs. We could only say thank you. I touched the women's shoulder and walked away in the twilight feeling sad, sad at not being able to help them in their poverty. They had been so kind to us.

The night was still and peaceful as we walked along. Both of us were silent. Two little boys were bathing in the river laughing and splashing one another. They stopped and waved at our passing. Ahead of us, a man was switching his cows across the trench and into his yard. We were in a different place in a different time ...

Charity felt comfortable. It was easy to settle in. On walks we took, people ran out to say hello, asking us questions and answering a few of ours in return. One of the school teachers introduced himself and asked about our schools and government.

We bought bread and juice at one of the stalls and met the owner, Audrey. She had two children. Her mother stayed with them because her husband was always in the bush mining gold. She invited us to her home to meet her mother. We sat outside on a bench (never seeing the inside) and drank more coconut milk and answered their questions.

They wanted to exchange money with us so they could make some purchases when they went to Georgetown because the

Guyanese currency was plummeting and unreliable. Many stores in Georgetown only used American currency. We could not chat for too long because our dialects were different and after speaking slowly and listening attentively, our concentration was short-lived.

In the steaming afternoons, we were immobile from the heat, so we sat upstairs in the small lobby and played Yahtzee. When we visited Lee's family, this was a common experience. His siblings and parents were great card players. They spent hours at the kitchen table throwing cards or dice and laughing. In the summer, it was an activity for camping, which they all did. I enjoyed their camaraderie and learned different card games, at which I became quite good. My family was more the board game type and not as boisterous. Anyway, as we were playing Yahtzee, an occasional bar customer would walk upstairs just to "look at the Americans" and smile or wave ... somehow the young boys 8-12 years of age always found us.

Soon we had taught six boys the game. They played against each other. Happy to learn a new activity, they squealed in excitement as they threw the dice, pushing on each other, laughing and yelling, their eyes bright and happy. One afternoon the manager thought the boys were making too much of a nuisance and threw them out.

We tried to explain it was fine with us, but I think he just didn't want the commotion.

Our new friend Phillip, who worked at the hotel, often came in to watch the boys. He helped us explain any nuances of the game since he could easily understand our English. After the boys were dismissed he spent some afternoons with us and told us his story. Phillip was a native of Georgetown: 25 years of age, slight, good looking and a blend of Black and Indian parents. He was a journalist for one of the Georgetown papers and did well for a few years, but lost his popularity by printing in the newspaper that "the increase in the poverty of the Guyanese was directly proportional to the increase in personal wealth of the men in high political office." Serious threats on Phillip's life followed and he left Georgetown in the middle of the night, ending up in Charity where he was presently a night watchman for the bar and restaurant.

His dream was to immigrate to Canada. His aunt was working on some relatives who lived in Toronto to find employment for him, but Phillip was impatient and felt maybe a quicker way would be for us to find him a wife in the U.S. He bragged about his skills as a cook and typist, and said his aunt was rich and he was sure that she would pay any woman well. But, he added, his wish was to never divorce but to remain at his wife's service forever with gratitude. Phillip felt he was handsome and sellable and gave us some photos to show our friends, "just in case." He begged us to at least try.

Anytime we were talking to Phillip, Pauleen the maid hung around. She always kept the staircase in full view. Then she could see the manager's head coming up the stairs before he could see her. If she caught sight of him, she quickly grabbed the broom to appear busy at work. Pauleen talked very fast and we continuously had to slow her down. She talked a lot with her hands and so between her animation and a few keywords, we generally got the gist of what she was saying.

Pauleen had a dream too: for her baby to have a future. She said only in America could her "little one" have a future. She begged us to take her child, thinking that customs might be careless and not catch us. Pauleen was grateful to the United States for shipping canned milk to Guyana for babies, but now, she said, the milk was being sold on the black market to those who could afford to buy it and the profits filled the pockets of the officials. She kept right on talking. Pauleen was an Amerindian, the first true inhabitant of the region. She had beautiful brown skin, coal-black hair, maybe weighed 100 pounds, and had very small features. Pauleen and her husband had two children. He supported her well and she was happy. One day, however, he didn't come back with his crew. She never knew why. Pauleen had heard he was dead and she'd heard he was alive. She finally moved in with her aunty.

Her aunty squatted in an empty house by the river. It was hers until she left it. Pauleen had joined her there. The hotel felt sorry for her and gave them any leftover food. Pauleen said she liked the house by the river and was excited because they had just strung an electric line with three outlets into their house, but "of course, we would never use three at once." They still cooked over an open fire under their house, which was off the ground on stilts. There was plenty of firewood to be found in the reeds on the bank of the river nearby.

Pauleen had worked at the hotel for a few years and had sworn off men. Except ... "One night there was a man from Venezuela so tempting and kind and he had the lightest of skin. I saw him just the one night but God must have meant it to be," she said. "He gave me a beautiful child, the fairest I have ever seen. We all adore her but my baby has no future here. Will you please take her with you?" We knew there was no way she could be without her child. Pauleen's devotion to her baby was so great her heart would have broken in two if the infant permanently left her side.

Even though the boys we had taught Yahtzee could no longer come up and see us in the hotel, they found us as we were walking around Charity and chatted away, following us for a while. One day, as we were walking down the road away from the village two of the boys came to get us. The taller one said, "Come on to the river and watch the boats come in. Tomorrow is market and everybody comes. Indians come to swap and miners come to sell gold, Many kids come too so we have lots of fun."

We all walked back to the river. Lee and I found a log that sat elevated on the highest part of the land ... a perfect spot to observe all the activity. Within minutes the boys were distracted and left us. We continued to watch the boats come in; some used motors but many were low riding dugouts containing families and produce. In one, the man was in the bow silent and paddling. The woman paddled in synchrony while monitoring the children sitting in front of her. When they got to shore, the boats were snuggly secured and their owners searched for a place on the bank to spend the night. Many tied their hammocks to trees onshore or to the frame of the pavilion that sat on the water's edge. It was late afternoon, and the place was coming to life. The momentum seemed to build with every boat that arrived onshore.

Two men in a rowboat came into the cove by the pavilion looking for a spot to tie up. Finally, they placed their anchor into the nearest boat and fastened the two boats together with the rope. There was a large bundle of laundry on the seat between them. Standing up, they lifted the bundle by a primitive rack they had constructed, each man taking one end. After getting help to come ashore, they began to walk down the road with people alongside and behind them.

We swung our legs over the log, turned our backs to the river and stepped up onto our log. What was the procession about? As I stood up, clinging to Lee's arm I noticed that the bundle had been "unfolded" and become a figure draped in a white sheet. I gasped and turned to Lee; it was a dead human being! The procession stopped and a few people stepped aside when two policemen appeared out of nowhere. The men set the stretcher on the ground; the police uncovered the body and rolled it over, poking at it the entire time. I could see people talking quietly among themselves. Shortly the dead man was rolled back over, covered once again and the entire group proceeded down the road.

When our young friends caught up with us later they told us the dead man lived alone far down the river. The two men, coming upriver to buy supplies, decided to paddle over and check on him and found the man lying dead outside his door. They brought him in for an examination since they suspected "foul play."

After the excitement of the dead man, we turned back to watching the parade of boats. Some were packed with bananas that were stacked in a pyramid shape, their bright lime green color a shocking contrast to the backdrop of the dark foliage of the river. It looked and felt like the jungle! There were many boats filled to the brim with coconuts; the loading system looked very precarious, as if the smallest jolt could cause an avalanche that could bury the oarsman. Unloading the coconuts was a ritual. It was not unlike an ant colony where all members knew their niches and moved in harmony. The first member pitched the coconut between his legs, like a football, to the next, who threw it up to the man on the dock, who dropped it into a burlap bag. When it was full, someone brought the bag to a human scale; a humongous obese man who stood with his arm outstretched holding a hook with a scale on top. After placing the bag on the hook, another man read the weight and wrote it down. Yet another man brought it over to a large truck, handing the sack up to someone who stood in the back of the truck stacking the bags until the trailer was filled to capacity, ready to drive to a barge at Supenaam (the point where we had crossed the river) and travel to Georgetown. We figured that either the Pomeroon River (Charity's location) was too narrow for barges, or too expensive; we never saw any large boats.

The activity at the harbor mesmerized us ... we had been sitting for hours. Our legs were cramped, but we were feeling the rhythm of rural Guyana. I wandered over to the pavilion to buy beverages, and then Lee went back and bought a few bananas. And we continued to sit, glued to our log trying to stay out of the way, fascinated by our surroundings. Some men walked by carrying cases, like portable typewriters. We followed them with our eyes and were surprised to see them stop, opening up their case to take out a small scale. The miners came up with gold and received dollars proportional to the weight of the gold. Were these buyers independent or did they all work for a BIG man? (Our question was never answered.)

Darkness settled in and the inhabitants under the pavilion lit their homemade kerosene lamps; bottles of all kinds with handmade braided wicks sticking out of the top. The wicks were smoking as they gave off their light. Some natives wandered in to buy food while others were lying in their hammocks being lulled to sleep by the background noises. The night was black and the smoking lights against the dark faces looked eerie and unearthly. Lee put his arm around me. "It's unreal," he said. "I'm so glad we came."

* * *

OUR DAY HAD COME to a close. We were exhausted from watching the activity and it was time to relinquish our post on the log and return to the hotel. Besides, tomorrow was the market, the highlight of the week.

The commotion outside our window woke us early the next morning. We quickly dressed and hurried out. Granted we had seen some weather-beaten stalls on a path next to the Xenon, but we assumed the market would be along the river. How wrong we were! Today the dilapidated stalls looked alive and content, dressed in tarps and goods of many colors. Tons of people had appeared from apparently nowhere and were swarming around buying, selling or looking.

We purchased some juice, biscuits, and bananas and browsed as we ate. Men were walking about with silvery fish on a string and crabs in a bucket singing, "Fish for sale." A lady displayed her vegetables in a bright and colorful way, showing sections of red peppers, green peppers, and halved eggplant with its purple skin and yellow seeded interior. It was a beautifully composed landscape picture, and all edible.

As we walked along the river there were boats three and four deep tied to one another. It was the only way to allow for a high volume of shoppers and traders. It felt like a carnival to us, but to the people of Charity and the surrounding area, it was a day to swap gossip and buy or sell merchandise. The sun was shining and everyone seemed to be enjoying the day.

Lee and I also traded with the merchants. I swapped a new yellow T-shirt with a lion on it for a handmade rug of material scraps, and Lee traded some books we had finished reading with the traveling librarian. No books could be bought outright; the idea was to have new books in circulation. With a book swap, a fee was added to support the librarian who hauled these books to every market.

Walking along, a persuasive, jolly salesman sold us some green peanuts, assuring us that with every peanut eaten we would gain more wisdom. We could not resist such an opportunity and after quite a few peanuts we had our first revelation: "We were very thirsty." First, we tried a fruit we had seen the locals eating that was the size of a small orange with brown skin. It was called a *sapodilla*. Mimicking their eating techniques, we pulled the skin back with our teeth and found a brown meaty fruit that tasted like a candied date. This was too sweet to quench our thirst so we ate a grapefruit next. It was the size of a melon and the interior was very coarse and full of seeds, but it was juicy and satisfied our thirst.

With sticky hands, Lee and I went to the river to wash up. We saw some Indians unloading rattan products to be sent to Georgetown for export. "Let's see if we can buy one," Lee whispered. Walking up, we each purchased a hat for one dollar. The sun was coming on with ferocity and we needed protection. Many women carried umbrellas, but to continuously take them down when there were so many people or to hold them high above their heads was a skill that was more difficult than it looked. On one occasion, I had attempted an umbrella but got sidetracked watching people and almost hit someone's face. I realized this was not going to make me a popular visitor! Wearing our hats, we stood in the shade of one of the trucks being loaded for Georgetown and watched the activity. It seemed the sexes divided the chores. The men went to fill any large containers: petro, kerosene, maybe cooking oil (even though they weren't as large) and then stopped to relax in the beer garden with their friends. After their wives had finished the rest of the shopping, men were to load their boat, unless, of course, they were too full of beer and then their wives would do that, too.

Most all groceries were bought in bulk: beans, peas, rice, flour, potatoes and fruit. The women felt and held the produce. Most of it was weighed on old-fashioned metal scales with two arms, one holding the weights and the other, the product. The women socialized between their purchases. Only their small children seemed discontent. They were pooped from chasing all their little friends for the last couple of hours and now it was hot and they were ready to receive attention and to go home. Their mothers placed them in the shade with some fruit or treat and went back to their buying. A few children wouldn't cooperate, but the majority were content and ready for a nap. It was a day of celebration for most, a change in routine and touching base with friends. How would they like to shop in our country? Would they trade their sociability for our vast goods at a supermarket?

Lee and I watched as people started to pack up and leave. We were beginning to feel the pulse of the Guyanese, but we also needed to make our way back to Georgetown to catch our plane. We hated to leave the little village of Charity and its warm and friendly people.

Our footsteps were hesitant and slow as we walked back to Xenon and up the steps to sit on our balcony one more time. Pauleen had left for the day, but Phillip came up to join us later. He brought three bottles of beer to toast us farewell. "Safe travels and please find me a wife," he said, lifting his bottle.

"Thanks, Phillip," Lee replied. "I hope someday you're as lucky as me."

"Carry my photos wherever you go," Phillip said, heading for the stairs.

"Take care," I said as he disappeared.

* * *

THE NEXT MORNING WE rose before the sun had come up and walked to the river in the cool darkness. The driver with the pink dash did not appear, but a small van came, which filled up quickly. As we were leaving, the sun started to rise from its bed and in the dim light, we saw Charity for the last time. Driving back, the sights of the rural people were familiar: children in uniform walking side-by-side to school, produce drying on the road, cows and goats grazing peacefully, and beautiful greenery and farms ... these images are forever imprinted on our minds.

The three-hour ride to the river went quickly and we were once again standing in front of the malaria warning. Lee purchased two bottles of orange soda for us to drink before leaving. Inhaling it, we waited. A half an hour later, a boat heading to Parika came, accompanied by wind. The driver said that he would only take 10 adults and 2 children because the water was rough, "very very rough," and less weight would be better. Fortunately, we were chosen to leave on the boat. All of a sudden someone was pointing at us. We thought we had to get out. But no, we still held our beverage bottles and they needed to be returned. We were embarrassed; the other riders understood and smiled or chuckled. Then our seatmates tucked the tarps around us. Our driver crossed himself and said a prayer, "Just one more time God I need Your help to safely reach the other side because the water is filled with fury." Crossing himself again, he started the motor and rode into the wind with our destinies captive in the wooden vessel.

I saw only two small life preservers on the floor for the children. And I felt the wind, the wind of our worst nightmares, the one which is strong and fearless against its foes. Was there a tornado or cyclone coming? The waves seemed like mountains! Why did our driver risk all our lives?

He stood stalwart at the stern, like a warrior in battle. Keeping the boat in the trough between two waves, he instinctively and aggressively charged through each wave into the next trough. His helper feverishly bailed the water that rushed in. But he could not keep up with the deluge. I held the tarp tightly under my chin awaiting the hurdle through the next wave and the water that poured down my chest. As I looked towards the distant and questionable shoreline, I only hoped that upon capsizing my adrenaline and sidestroke would carry me to shore. I told Lee to save himself as I kept my eyes open, wishing I was more religious ... then my prayers to stay alive might be answered. I was suspended in the moment as the water hit my chest and my future looked uncertain.

Suddenly the winds stopped as if they were controlled by an on/off switch. The driver sat down and the helper quit bailing ... had I not been sopping wet I would have questioned that the fierce winds had ever existed.

* * *

WHEN OUR BOAT DOCKED in Parika, the winds were spent and the waters calm. Two boys recognized us from last time and waved and smiled until the boat docked. They helped us ashore. "Come on, you take my cousin's car to Georgetown. He gives you good ride," the smaller boy said. Lee and I walked up the shore to the market, on solid ground, elated to once again feel the coconut shells and peelings crunching beneath our feet. The two boys insisted we sit in the best seat, in front with the driver, and shook our hands like we were their friends. Lee and I thanked them, assuring them we had a wonderful time. As we drove away, the boys were jumping up and down waving and yelling. The sun splashed its light through the window onto Lee's red shirt as though it were a celestial kiss.

And Lee and I leaned against each other and felt the warmth around us ...

* * *

Arriving in Georgetown in mid-afternoon, we returned to the Tower Hotel for a room. We wanted to spend the remainder of the day looking for a memento and having dinner before our return home. On our way out of the door, the guard at the hotel said to stay on the boulevard and not to wander off on the side streets, as they were not safe. Nodding, we walked down the boulevard and went to the market we had visited before, stopping on the way to thank Ronald. We were disappointed he wasn't there, but his sister promised to relay our message.

Not seeing many crafts at the market, we walked to the store-fronts, a few blocks away. We found a shop, established by the Catholic Church, which gave all its profits to unwed mothers. Lee and I found a mahogany carved relief of a mother and child. Leaving the store with our newspaper-wrapped purchase, we noticed a neon sign flashing a few blocks over, in an upstairs window, advertising Chinese food. After seating ourselves, Lee ordered a chicken dish and I, still skittish from my food poisoning in Charity, ordered soup and rice. With happy stomachs, we retraced our steps, down the stairs.

Lee took my hand. "I think this is the way to the Tower Hotel," he said. Within a few blocks, we were walking in the most impoverished area I have seen in my entire life. We attempted to look straight ahead and didn't talk. The dilapidated sign of "Malaria Kills" and the words, "The hospital is a place to go to die," flashed through my mind. Phillip's fear for his future and Pauleen's for her child resonated, too. I scanned the landscape. The dirt (no longer a lawn) around the dilapidated buildings was so worn it was as hard as a ceramic pot. Dismantled cars and trash decorated the area. Children in tattered clothes stood watching us, as though we were aliens. For a few seconds, I locked eyes with a man sitting on a barrel. I saw hunger and desperation in his eyes. He looked as hungry as a dying tiger in the wilds, too weak to attack his prey. My heart ached! This was the second time in twenty-four hours I wanted to pray, only this time for the Guyanese ...

We kept walking and eventually came out on the boulevard. Relieved, we found our way back to the hotel and went to our room. That night, I slept in Lee's arms until I was awakened by a sound. I thought someone was trying to break in. I got up and using the dial phone contacted the guard. After investigating, he found it was a misfiring air conditioner in the next room.

I didn't go back to sleep. My mind was stuck in a haunting unbroken loop questioning how many Guyanese knew hope and opportunity ...

1997

Ecuador

❧

It matters not how strait the gate,
How charged with punishments the scroll,
I am the master of my fate,
I am the captain of my soul.

—**William Ernest Henley**
Invictus

CHAPTER ONE

Quito

A dventure is in my blood, curiosity my eighth sense. It cannot be restrained. Travel had always been a diversion; a pleasurable respite from routine. Weekly, our friend Hazel saved the travel section from her newspaper and brought it to us. Systematically, I checked the bargains, followed up with calls to the airlines, researched possibilities and hoped for a miraculous deal. In September, I hit the jackpot, finding two one-half price tickets to Quito, Ecuador, for the following February.

Finally, we were flying over the ocean on our way to Quito and vistas unknown. Lee and I just received our dinners on a flight due to arrive at 10 p.m. I was given a Kosher meal; he a vegetarian. Over the years I have ascertained that any special meal was better prepared than the usual fare, but this flight proved me wrong. "Sorry, Lee," I said as I watched him unwrap yellow squash, tofu and a piece of cornbread. "Here, take my turkey. I'm a lot smaller than you, you'll be starved."

"We won't look too serious about our diets if we switch our plates back and forth," he answered taking the turkey and giving me his cornbread. "I'm not sure about your strategy on airplane food service," he said glancing at the tray to the left of me which contained a nice portion of chicken.

I turned to the young woman beside me and said, "Usually it works to try something different."

She smiled in reply.

After eating, I opened my book to read. I was restless and not able to concentrate. The movie the airline was showing wasn't of interest either, but the conversation behind me was; a male steward was flirting with two young females who were on their way home from the U.S. They were bilingual and conversing in English. Their short skirts and halter tops encouraged his continued interest.

I struck up a conversation with the gal next to me whose name was Rita, and found that she had a position in Riobamba, south of Quito to teach English. "I didn't feel like finishing college so I took a class at a Berlitz school and became a certified Spanish/English teacher. A friend of mine with the Peace Corps in Ecuador gave me the idea. I've never been out of the state of Idaho before, but it felt like time. My parents were really upset. Fortunately, I had enough savings for a ticket and left. Hopefully, they will adjust."

"Is your friend meeting you at the airport?"

"I'm not sure. She told me to stay at the youth hostel called Moby the Grape. She may already be there depending on her schedule. If not, I'll just hang out for a few days before leaving for Riobamba. I'm sure she'll catch up with me sooner or later."

"Do you have an address for the hostel? We've made a reservation at a hotel and requested that they send someone to pick us up. Maybe we could drop you off."

Taking her info and our lodging confirmation, I turned around and sweetly interrupted our loquacious steward. The girls seemed to be losing interest and were probably relieved to have another distraction. "Yes," one girl answered, "they are near each other so you could take the same car."

I felt pleased that we could help Rita out. With our flight arrival scheduled so late, I could tell she felt more comfortable getting into Quito now that she had company.

After going through customs we went out to look for our ride. The people waiting were very quiet and docile, not the usual clamor and noise that is part of arrival at most airports. Lee and I looked around for a sign with our names on it. We waited for another 15 minutes, but no one appeared.

"So much for my great idea," I said.

Rita, using her newly learned Spanish, found us a cab. The price quoted was a few dollars each. We got into the car and were off to find our rooms. Driving up to Moby the Grape, a woman stood waiting by the steps.

"That's my friend," Rita said.

In cheerful spirits, we drove away. Everything was closed and quiet. Most of the area was commercial. Then we turned a corner. The military was parading back and forth, guns upon their shoulders.

"What's going on?" I asked in clumsy Spanish.

"A police station," he answered.

It sounded rather suspicious to me. He turned the corner and tried to approach the hotel from two different directions, but the streets were blocked. "I think we have to learn more Spanish than menus and asking for directions," Lee said. "Didn't you call the embassy?"

"Yes, but that was before I bought the tickets. Obviously, something has happened since then."

Finally, we drove up in front of our hotel. After paying the driver, we walked into the lobby. The clerk on duty did not know of our arrival. His English was nonexistent. I showed him our confirmation and explained, in Pidgin Spanish, that we needed a room.

He pulled a matching form from a box on the desk. Wiping his brow he said it was in the book for tomorrow and he did not have the promised room over the park with a balcony but there was one room left in the back.

The guidebook that had listed the hotel had not checked its sources either for a long time or never. The facade wasn't bad, but the interior was in disrepair. The only reason we decided to stay was the parading military close to our hotel. The room was damp, filthy and had such a dirty sofa that we sat on our jackets as we discussed our dilemma. The light on the nightstand was bolted down, but we could still change the bulb with the higher wattage we had brought with us (always part of our inventory). We sat on the bed, leaned against the wall, and sharing the light, read until our eyes closed. Fortunately, between one another's body heat and the one blanket, we slept through the damp cold night.

The same clerk was on duty the next morning. We paid him without comment, and much to his disappointment, we walked out the door in search of another place. Close by we found the Amaranta Internacional Hotel which was less expensive than the previous evening. They gave us a room on the fourth floor which included a refrigerator plus a sitting room and a huge window with a spectacular view of the city and mountains. We couldn't believe our good fortune!

Deciding to explore, we went back downstairs to ask the concierge questions. She was distracted and dismissive. However, she handed us a map of the city highlighting our present location and circling the areas we should explore. Since she wasn't of much help, we went in search of breakfast and a city tour to see the old section of Quito (which was said to be beautiful). Plus, we needed to find an explanation for the procession of the military outside our door.

The first agency said, "No tours today."

The second said, "Fifty dollars per person. The tour leaves in ten minutes. Here's a list of ongoing tours with a map of the region on the back. This is our last tour today. The others won't resume until the strike is over." We took our literature and left, not eager to drop $100 on a tour within 24 hours of arrival.

The third told us that they were not having any tours because many of the buildings were closed. "Government problems," they said. The agent told us to catch a cab and just walk around. "There is military presence because of the pending strike," she said as the phone rang. "One moment," she replied into the receiver and then turned to assure us we would be safe and not to worry, dismissing us with a wave of her hand.

Walking a few blocks further we found a place called Cafe' Cultura, which served breakfast, sandwiches and coffee. They also had a few rooms to rent ... I'd call them a deluxe hostel. The person at the front desk, introducing himself as Mateo, had extremely good English. He related the political situation. "We have had a president here for only six months. At first the people, they love him. But the man turned crazy. We call him El Loco. He lives fancy and robs the people. In the short time he is president, the gasoline prices go up so high. To some people, they are double since he comes. No longer do we want him. Our union leader has told us to strike on Wednesday, close our shops and go home and pray that he will no longer rule us. Our representatives said they will help us and have a meeting and get rid of him, but only if we are serious and strike. But people are fearful of riots and do not know how to prepare for this."

Lee and I thanked Mateo for educating us. We sat in the dining room and drank very strong coffee and ate their homemade bread and marmalade. Lee opened the map he had just received from the travel agent. We had no other literature with us; our travel book was back at the hotel. "Here's a rough map of Ecuador," Lee said pointing to the area south of Quito. "Our original plan was to go down to Latacunga for the market, then to Banos, ending up still further south in Azogues to see the Incan ruins [Lee was into the history of ruins]. There's a lot to do around Azogues and Cuenca. If possible, we were going to stop at Riobamba on the way back. Now it sounds like everything is changed and we'd better move quickly. Why don't we head for one of the cities on our original plan?"

"Good idea. Let's leave early tomorrow. I'd rather be in the country if we have to get stuck somewhere."

"I agree, sweetie," Lee answered. We sat and had another cup of coffee looking out the window and discussing our plans.

Before leaving, we asked Mateo to call a few contacts we had: one, a coffee farmer who our friends knew from the Peace Corp; another, a sister of an exchange student of a California cousin. He tried both numbers and left messages telling them where we were staying presently and that we would return there before leaving for the States. Since Mateo didn't seem to mind our questions, I showed him the map and asked him which town we should head for. "Banos would be good," he said. "The town is small and isolated and you'd be safe there."

As Lee was paying and tipping him for making the calls, I asked Mateo's advice once again. "Should we walk around the old city this afternoon or explore the neighborhood around our hotel?"

Mateo put the money in the register before answering. "The people here are very peaceful. Ecuadorians are very cosmopolitan and no one will even know you are not local if you don't carry a camera or tourist gear. Take a cab over and walk around. It is a beautiful city. Enjoy yourselves." We smiled and parted.

Lee and I discussed our dilemma on the way back to the Amaranta.

"Why not walk around, "Lee said. "After all, both parties said it was OK. And Mateo said that we wouldn't be noticed or bothered."

Returning to the hotel, we put our passports and money in flat pouches attached to our underwear; any other gear was left behind. In my purse I carried a few dollars, our airline tickets and the city map our hotel had given us.

We walked away from our military-patrolled corner, found a cab and rode over to the old city. Few words were exchanged since our Spanish was minimal and slowly spoken so most cannot understand it. Our driver finally stopped, pointed down the street, and told us to follow it and we would walk into the square. "It is too crowded to drive more," he said.

After paying, we jumped out of the cab to seek our destiny. We walked with the people down a narrow street heading towards the square. Street vendors lined the sidewalks in little stalls hoping to sell their merchandise as the masses walked by.

There was some discussion among neighboring merchants and passersby, none of which could be interpreted quickly enough by our ears. We kept moving along, caught in the cadence of those around us, our feet in tempo to the words "El Loco" echoing through the air.

As we walked into the square we realized, while meant with good intent, that the suggestion that we should walk around and explore was perhaps said with tongue-in-cheek to promote a warm welcome. Lee and I looked at each other with discomfort.

I whispered to him, "We definitely should not be here!" The environment was very somber. It was a square, like many in the world, with buildings surrounding a large courtyard and fountain normally occupied by sparsely populated benches, stalls or carts of friendly vendors and resident pigeons.

But today the scene was different. It mirrored the unrest in Ecuador. The military was plentiful and very obvious. The white helmets, green uniforms and guns reminded people to watch their behavior. Plastic netting covered the facades of the government buildings. It was attached at the roofline and dropped to the ground, leaving breathing room between the building and the net to feign some protection against rocks, paint bombs or objects that could mar their aged and weathered stone faces.

People were huddled on the benches talking softly to one another while others stood watching. The more active walked up and down with signs or stood looking toward the administrative buildings as though waiting for someone specific to come or go, or for any kind of action.

The atmosphere was filled with discontent: clouds of unrest and disenchantment with El Loco filled the air. No one seemed to know what to do. The union leaders who had organized and posted the signs must have had a plan, but the people appeared confused and out of their element. To make a faster retreat, we walked diagonally across the square, not feeling fear but timidity.

Lee and I scurried along, but could still see a military member escort a person into the building. We observed the worried faces around us, and exited at the opposite corner of the square, relieved to be removed from the drama. Our quandary now was how to return to the newer part of the city. We walked in haste toward a familiar-looking tall building in the far distance.

The traffic was dense, the hour busy. Buses sputtered, expelling black clouds of flatulent pollution from their tailpipes. Through open windows we saw people clinging to the overhead bars while the others stood packed in the aisles like kernels on a corn cob, waiting to burst out of their confinement.

The pollution was the likes of which I have never seen. An endless parade of buses loaded with military, workers and shoppers roared past, their oily black bituminous belches trailing behind. Lee and I kept walking, deciding that since we did not know the bus lines it would be an unwise attempt to use intuition. We saw no cabs in sight.

Finally, we took out our map to get our bearings and walked on in the smoggy daylight. "We have to keep moving," I said. "Our heads are not used to this stuff in the air. Unreal, isn't it? I have never felt pollution sting my eyes and make my head feel like it was going to explode."

It was a long walk down seemingly endless streets, first through the old section, then across a large park and finally into the newer section of town. We returned tired and hungry to our hotel, our feet sore from the miles we had walked.

A new clerk was on duty when we arrived and introduced herself as Danielle, offering to help us in any way. We asked her to describe the mood of the country and wanted to know if we were in any danger.

Dannielle's English was impeccable and she seemed interested in talking; she was not busy and updated us with the news. "Our hotel services are already slowing down, two days early," she said. "A strike is scheduled for Wednesday but everyone wants to be organizing their homes to get ready. The hotel dining room is closed for that reason. People are out shopping to buy groceries and to prepare. All merchants are asked to close down and the country is supposed to stop to show El Loco that we will not put up with his disregard for our lives. He has violated our trust and tripled the cost of electricity and fuel. We can take it no longer. I just spoke with my brother, who is a city worker and he says that the government has made the gas stations close around Quito so fuel cannot be purchased. They do not want to encourage transportation around the city or country to enable the people to riot. You must stay here until the strike is over. Your room is comfortable and you will be safe here."

On the long walk back to the hotel, we discussed our dilemma and reached our own conclusion. Lee looked directly at Danielle and replied. "We thought we'd try for Banos very early tomorrow. We would much rather be in a small town, does that sound possible?"

If there is no gasoline, I don't know if you'll make it out."

I interrupted, "Lee and I decided that we'll leave very early and take a cab right over to the bus terminal. If we can't catch a bus for Banos or anywhere else that interests us we'll be back. Can you save our room until 2 o'clock? We'll surely know by then."

Danielle thought we should remain in Quito but she agreed to our plan, nevertheless.

After freshening up we went back out to find someplace to eat. The streets were quiet and we finally found a Chinese restaurant open. Relieved, we ate. There were only two other tables occupied. The owner's wife had brought their small child. They sat at the front watching the register while reading books and playing paddy-cake. It was a lovely interlude in our evening.

Danielle was still at the desk when we returned. "Call the desk for a cab right when you get up. I wish you good luck. Most people here are peace-loving so you should be alright. Please come back if you do not find a way out."

Thanking her for her hospitality and advice, we returned to our room. We got our books and a drink, and we went up a small set of stairs onto the rooftop of the hotel. Finding a few chairs, we sat and looked over the city at the buildings and mountains surrounding the valley where Quito resided. Lee lifted his glass, "To an interesting vacation. May we be safe."

I looked at Lee. "You're the best," I said clinking glasses and giving him a kiss. He was a great traveler: rarely flustered, and an inquisitive soul. We'd been together 17 years and had weathered it well … opened a business plus remodeled and moved to the third floor of our duplex to ensure financial security. Then after ten years, moved down to the second floor only to look over our balcony railing and view drug dealing on our street—which precipitated selling and buying a small bungalow. Granted, we had a foreign exchange student living in our lower level to help with the rent, but we loved it. Plus, living in a house with a yard, I started raising dahlias and writing more and Lee started bicycling and repairing bikes because we were near a park with a lot of trails. Plus we were still working on the cabin next to our screen house. Life felt good and even through the veil of pollution and the atmosphere of political unrest, the city nestled snuggly in the mountains looked beautiful and serene.

We toasted again, to us and to the Ecuadorians. We hoped that their country would remain peaceful as they confronted change …

CHAPTER TWO

Banos

Dressing as the sun peered over the mountains, we were ready before our alarm sounded. We walked out of the hotel as the clock in the lobby read 6:30. A cab was waiting by the front door. After asking the fare, we jumped in and were off.

This was very unlike Lee and me since with our limited assets and interest in adventure we usually walked or took the local buses to get the feel of the place. But this morning our interest was different: to get out of Quito! We both felt that if there would be problems, it would be in the more densely populated cities, since the larger the gathering, the greater the chance for any spark to ignite the coals of unrest.

Our early rising brought us good luck. As we walked up to the window to buy our bus tickets we asked the salesgirl for Banos. "Un minuto," she said, holding up her finger and running out to yell at a bus backing out of the gate. The driver waited while we purchased our tickets, then we climbed aboard and left the terminal.

Driving down the road into the sunrise, we were soon riding in the country with Quito behind us. After a few hours, we transferred at Ambato, changing to a bus traveling southeast towards Banos. Across from us sat a woman from Sweden headed for the same place. She was on the bus because the train which she had planned on taking was canceled due to the impending strike.

When we arrived in Banos, we went our separate ways. She already knew of a hotel for $5 a night that was supposed to be clean and acceptable but we thought we'd explore our options first.

* * *

THE SQUARE WAS DESOLATE; quiet and empty of all vendors. The only visible activity was an ice cream man shouting, *"Helado, helado,"* as he pushed his cart. Walking by two cab drivers one said, "No work, we on strike."

We approached a store with a sign in the window which read "Tourist Maps." The door stood open but all was quiet. We took a free map and walked back onto the street.

"Wow," Lee said. "I guess Danielle was right. We were lucky to get here."

"Let's find a place to have coffee, read our travel book and check out all possible lodging. It looks like we're going to be here for a while. It might be wise to stay at a place where they serve food, in case all the restaurants close."

With the "basics" in mind, we sat down to study our new map and list of lodging in Banos. Some places were indexed on our map. We noticed that Quito was 176 km away, which accounted for the hours it had taken us.

Starting our exploration, we stopped at a place on the square which had a clean room with a private bath and hot water plus a rooftop with a few chairs to catch some breeze. The price: $5. It seemed unbelievable to find such value so we walked along to check on what else was available. For $7 we found a place that served food, had a small lounge with wooden chairs, and in addition had a garden with monkeys and parrots. The room was clean but we had to share a bath. My concern was if all were quiet, and we spent a lot of time reading and lounging at our hotel, it would be nice if there were a few chairs with cushions vs. straight hard-back chairs.

"Let's find something really comfortable and see what that would cost," I said.

There were a fair number of places to choose from. We finally decided on Monte Selva, accommodations with fifteen little A-frame cabins nestled on the hill. To access the cabins, steep steps dug into the earth with planks implanted on them joined the levels. The view was spectacular! Of course, with three precipitous tiers of steps to climb to get to our cabin, our goal was never leave anything in the room that we had to retrieve. The price was $28 a night and they did serve food. We were told there was only one other cabin rented besides ours.

The hotel clerk, Maria, was very friendly and had better English than our Spanish. We tried to teach one another words as she kept us abreast of the political situation. She was displeased with the new edict that there should be no road travel, and even more displeased with the fact that activists of the local areas were blocking roads to their towns and villages.

"Now we will have no tourists. They cannot arrive here if they want, so we cannot charge them for not coming. But we must all sacrifice something to get rid of El Loco."

We explored Banos on foot. There was neither a cab driver to be hired nor a bus that moved. We could see the vehicles being washed and shined but there was no transportation to be found. Private vehicles moved around and few restaurants and stores were open for limited hours. Normally, Banos had tourists. We looked for a bicycle shop. Lee was excited when he found one. It listed the tours on a big chalkboard. Using his best Spanish, Lee tried to rent bikes but no deal. They were striking with Ecuador. Lee was disappointed.

"Wow, some of their mountain bike trips looked great and we could've seen the country," he said.

But Banos remained drowsy, and most of it slept while awaiting the government to change. Fortunately, our feet and legs were healthy and strong because they were our only "wheels." Many sites around Banos interested us, but since the volcanoes, parks, waterfalls and reserves were miles away, we were out of luck. In town, we walked everywhere possible. There was a small museum we found open one day; a hot spring and bath were closed because of the strike, but the nearby waterfalls had a sheltered set of troughs filled with the water where we watched women pounding their laundry.

The little boys in the park played marbles for hours. I even captured them in one of the rare photos I took (which unfortunately

I gave to my cousin, an avid marble collector). We walked as many of the winding trails as we could, passing burros heavily laden with supplies in baskets, and people without the luxury of a four-legged animal tying those same heavy baskets onto their backs.

One day we passed a small building with three burros outside. Why were they there? There was no sign on the facade to give us a clue.

We walked by homes and businesses with televisions, and many times the screen showed commentators or a view of Quito and the masses on the square. Our hotel clerk was optimistic. "I know that they will solve it by the weekend because Mardi Gras is our biggest festival of the year, and nothing will stand in the way of our celebration."

Maria convinced us and we were comforted. She also told us that El Loco had escaped on a private plane and no one knew where he went and that the vice president initially supported him so he was not to be trusted to preside. Meanwhile, all the representatives were in a locked room discussing who should rule until the next election.

Already, congress had voted El Loco out of power. Only a majority of votes were needed if the president was considered "mentally incompetent," and two-thirds if it were for other reasons. El Loco was in the former category and quickly voted out. However, the citizens would continue to strike until they knew the fate of their leadership.

* * *

LEE AND I CONTINUED to explore the terrain. We walked to a beautiful cemetery up on a hill where the monuments were huge and luxurious. Most of the headstones had a built-in enclosed glass-covered shelf, lit with Christmas lights, which housed favorite memorabilia and photos. Extension cords ran along the ground and over the stones as though they were invisible to the human eye. We studied the collection of objects in the showcases, discussing what they might mean and which families were the most nostalgic and who was loved the most. One showcase had many great family pictures and said: "El Abuelo" (grandfather). Lee stood in front of the case and said, "Look. This man was the same age as my dad."

I hugged him. "Sorry, Dad was wonderful." Before we moved into our bungalow both Lee's dad and our dog, Sunshine, had died. It was the only time I ever saw Lee cry. He idolized his father and loved the dog that he had walked daily for years.

But this day was sunny, and the bright plastic flowers and whitewashed stones gave the cemetery a happy feeling. When the music suddenly came on through the loudspeakers we felt like we were at a festival honoring the dead. The music must have been on a timer, or maybe it was morning music for the slumbering spirits to dance and socialize. It felt like we were intruders stumbling into their world for a short visit.

Maria was just arriving as we walked up to Mount Selva. "Maria," I said. "We love your cemetery. It is so festive."

She laughed. "Come back in early November when we celebrate All Saints Day and Day of the Dead. Families bake bread in the shape of human and animal figures. They leave food and drink by the graves of their loved ones to encourage them to come back to earth and visit them. Then others less fortunate or hungry come and offer prayers, and in return eat and drink the gifts. It is a very festive time."

* * *

WALKING UP AND DOWN the steep hills of Banos we felt content and physically fit. Maria assured us that the strike would be over and we could see more of her country before we needed to return to the States. What more did we need to be concerned about? There were enough restaurants open, we had a comfortable place to stay and we could always swap our books at any other hotel (it was common practice to have a shelf to exchange read-books for no cost).

One day we felt particularly ambitious and decided to hike to the zoo or "animal prison" as it was so labeled on our map. It was a two-mile hike, and all uphill. As we left the city we passed two entrance roads into Banos, both had a pile of smoldering tires on the road so that no vehicle could pass. Lee and I looked at one another, dismayed at the sight.

It was one thing to hear the news of the impassability and another to see. Eyes cannot lie.

To have witnessed the masses at the square in Quito seemed like an isolated event, but seeing the smoldering tires in front of us changed the picture. It was not a feeling of fear that spread through my being, but one of encroachment and the certainty that unrest had pervaded the country.

Hopefully, Maria was right and that Mardi Gras would be the motivation to end the strike. Fortunately, we had our little cabin to await the changing of events.

Silently, we walked up the street to the "animal prison." The road turned sharply to the right and crossed a small river to get up the hill to the zoo; on the riverbank stood a shrine with St. George spreading his hands as though protecting the natives against the terror of high water. We kept walking up the steep hill wondering if there even was a zoo. It surely seemed like an out-of-the-way place.

A private car passed us. We both were realizing that we would have to walk back and the sun was getting stronger every minute. I put my umbrella up and started grumbling. "Is this hot or what? I wonder what animals can survive in this sun. I sure hope someone is selling something cool to drink up there."

Lee laughed. "I agree. I doubt our oranges and coconut macaroons will do the trick in this heat. Whose idea was this anyway?"

"Ours," I replied. "Besides, we felt like an adventure today, remember?"

Arriving at our destination two-thirds of the way up the hill, we saw the zoo on the right side sitting on top of a cliff with the road continuing still higher into the mountains.

"There's supposed to be a waterfall around here somewhere," I said.

"Let's talk about it as we sit on those stools over there. It looks as though we can even get a beverage," Lee said.

After we sat down, a man came out of his house. "Can I help you?" he asked.

"Yes," answered Lee, "two cerveza."

When he returned, we asked if there was anyone to get a ride down the hill with. "No taxi," he said, and shrugged as to the possibility of catching a ride with anyone else.

Eating our macaroons and drinking our beer, Lee and I looked around. The gift shop was closed, there were no vehicles parked anywhere but someone sat by the ticket booth. Was it the salesperson or another visitor just lounging?

Feeling cooled down and revived, we sauntered over to find out. The person scurried into the hut to sell us tickets. Lee paid, and we followed the walkway to explore.

The zoo was situated right on top of a precipitous stone mountain, exposed to the sun, rain and any other elements in the area. Umbrella overhead, we walked up and down a zillion stairs and looked at any birds or animals that chose to remain in the sun. Scattered around were small plots of flowers and cactus to show off the local flora.

Steps took us straight down the side of the hill to look at the monkeys and the turtles and back up another way to find ourselves at a lookout overhanging the water and the Ines Maria Falls in the near distance. It was a spectacular sight!

"Wow! After all this exercise we'll be ready for a marathon," Lee said.

"We just did one," I replied. "In fact, it wouldn't bother me at all if we found a ride back to our hotel."

Retracing our steps, we were coming out the entrance when a van arrived.

"Hey, maybe that's our ride," I said. And we watched as eight people got out.

"Nice try," Lee responded.

Sitting on the stools again, we waited, just in case a possibility drove by, but none came. We started walking down the hill retracing our journey up the hill.

"How about splurging on a nice dinner tonight to celebrate our stamina and good humor?" I asked.

"Great idea."

We never saw a car that afternoon. A horse and rider trotted by, and a woman led a burro wearing heavy baskets on his back. So, using our legs, we returned to Banos and looked for a place to eat.

Our decision was based on the "volume of tables occupied."

We had three choices and settled on the restaurant that had a TV on a high corner shelf. The employees were standing looking up at the screen watching the news and the first three tables in front of the screen were occupied with customers facing each other silently eating or drinking and watching the telecast of their history.

No one was talking; they were listening to the gentleman on the screen standing by the podium. I listened too and watched the faces of the restaurant customers. Their eyes were focused on the television, all expressions "on hold" until the message was delivered.

Then smiles appeared, talking erupted among the people and cheers came from the mouths of a few. The strike was over! Business was to resume. The content of the telecast was that after El Loco had been removed by the Ecuadorian Congress for his "mental incapacity," three people wanted to claim the presidency. Congress had just chosen and sworn in its new leader Fabian Alcaron—until the next election when the Ecuadorians could vote for their choice.

The televised square in Quito was filled with people clapping and banners waving. Their organized efforts were rewarded; the sacrifices made by the citizens had paid off. I was happy for the people, yet, had no idea what it cost each one of them.

It was impressive that the people had stuck together to cause change and that the system was able to respond so quickly and peacefully. It's difficult to believe that Mardi Gras was the true reason for their expediency, but it hardly mattered. They had resolved the dilemma quickly.

"I wonder if we can leave tomorrow," Lee said.

"Let's ask Maria when we get back, maybe she can call."

After dinner, we walked up and down the streets of Banos. Yes, we were tired from our walk to the zoo, but we felt energized with the end of the strike. We could tell that the people in Banos did too.

The boys in the park appeared to be rowdier in the marble game ... the atmosphere was more festive this evening. People were walking around and not glued to their TVs. Radios were blaring and the pace had quickened as though an anesthetic fog had moved away from the town.

Maria was friendly and excited when we got back to our cabin. "What did I tell you?" she said. "We will have our visitors for Mardi Gras." She beamed with expectation.

"Do you think the buses will run tomorrow?" I asked.

"The roads have to be cleared first so I doubt there will be much travel tomorrow. But I will call for you in the morning."

Thanking her we walked up to our cabin, pleased at the possibility of moving along and seeing more of Ecuador. We sat on our chairs outside; the lights below looked friendly, glimmering in pleasure at the good fortune of the residents.

CHAPTER THREE

Cuenca

When we checked out, Maria was not at the front desk. From our meager Spanish, we found that she had been thrown from her horse the evening before and wasn't feeling too well. Disappointed that we missed her, we left her a gift (a crocheted trivet that my mother made) along with a note, expressing our thanks and best wishes for her recovery. Then we walked away from our cabin and down the road to the bus station.

Arriving at the window, Lee asked for the schedule and cost to Cuenca, further south in the country. The salesperson didn't think there would be any buses going that day, but said to check back. We walked across the street, ate breakfast and had some coffee, and returned to the station for any news.

After still finding no possible transportation, we walked around Banos one more time, buying some bakery and juice, trying to think positively about getting out of the town. An hour later, checking one more time, we found a bus loading. The driver was doing it on his own, not through the bus lines, and would take us as far as he could. Within 45 minutes, the bus was packed and overloaded and on its way out of the square.

The first stop was by the smoldering tires Lee and I had walked by the day before. Two men (apparently the driver's helpers) got out and rolled enough tires away to allow him to pass on the shoulder. Nine-tenths of the tires remaining, he cautiously drove by, hoping not to end up in the ditch or caught in the rubble.

This was an easy feat in comparison to what was on the horizon. Within a few minutes, we approached a pile of huge limbs in the center of the road. Small branches locked the limbs together and made it impassable or immovable. Someone had the idea that we get out of the bus and collect all available branches and stones so the driver could use the ditch as his road. Two men had brought their machetes and cut larger pieces to form a base. Everyone was talking among themselves, deciding that together we could solve any impasse. Their spirit was refreshing but the question was, "Would we ever reach our destination?"

We left Banos at 10 am. Theoretically, the ride to Azogues, where we were headed, was to take six hours. Maybe there was someplace else we could layover. This was going to be a long day.

* * *

THE PASSENGERS WERE TENACIOUS; their high spirits infectious. We got out of the bus countless times, using our brains and brawn to solve the problem. We knew this would go down in our diary and storytelling as a great adventure of our lives.

Then we saw a humongous dead tree blocking the road. It had been severed from its place on the precipice above and tumbled top first into the ditch, with the trunk landing across our path. Was there no solution but to have Paul Bunyan and his ox Blue magically appear and help us out? We were rescued, once again by creative thinking. First, the truck ahead of us went around and then we followed.

Our driver persevered for a few miles before the road narrowed and a boulder, along with a tree had been pushed off the neighboring cliff onto our path. We were now at an impasse. Everyone scratched their head. Finally, an idea resulted. There was a side road about a mile back where we could take a cutoff. However, there was no way to turn around. "No problem," the driver said. He boarded all of us and started backing down the road.

His skill was phenomenal. Slowing around the bends and down the hill he backed until we safely arrived at the cutoff. Everyone cheered! We were on our way again.

The day continued in this fashion. The riders remained enthusiastic. Men, women and children got on and off to move the tires and branches or to push the bus. Nothing seemed too big or too large to conquer.

The countryside was some of the most beautiful that I have ever seen. The terrain was steep and very green. Their major product is coffee and we could see workers tending their plants in their bright-colored shawls and blond straw hats, hoeing away like they were on flat ground. It appeared to be about a 65-degree angle and looked as though if they turned around quickly they would fall face down and tumble to the bottom. We could see people working all the way up the mountain, like the builders on a skyscraper, with earthen shelves as their scaffolding.

Later, we came to a stop in the road. Men and women were sitting on logs and stones blocking the entrance to their village. "You cannot go there," they said. "The rebels are dropping rocks onto vehicles from overlooking points and we cannot stop them. We wanted to warn you because your bus would be harmed."

Our driver was a good soul but he shook his head in disbelief. None of the passengers could argue with him.

As we were about to turn around, a vehicle came over the side of a hill to the left of us. The road was very narrow; I thought it was a "path."

Getting out the driver talked to them and they said that the road was passable. They had just driven up and around, and that it would join our road a few miles down.

The driver talked to his helpers and everyone argued among themselves. The road was very narrow and not for buses, but now that we had come this far why should we turn back? The discussion ended with a collection of another 25 cent contribution for the gas and difficulty of the road.

The driver shifted into gear, and the riders cheered. The people got off of their logs and stones, moved them aside and we drove through and started up the trail on the hill.

In retrospect, it was insane. But the gods were with us because up the road we drove. I was sitting by the window. There was no shoulder; we were filling the road. Somehow I hoped that the three wheels would carry us if soft earth disappeared below a fourth.

The travelers were very quiet, especially on the stretch where there was no way anyone could pass and no shoulder was alongside us with a 100 food drop at our side. One woman was closing her eyes and moving her lips, pushing the beads of her rosary between her fingers.

After we arrived at the top of the hill the bus driver saw a man walking and asked him if the road ahead was as treacherous. He didn't seem to know, but how could it be any worse?

We kept moving and the road was less steep, although still narrow. We never met or saw anyone driving on the road, which was the greatest miracle of all.

Coming down the hill we could see people sitting on rocks blocking the entrance to the road and a bus sitting in the opposing position, the same quandary we confronted an hour before.

We cheered as we saw our road, and as we stopped the bus drivers exchanged pleasantries. Our bus driver was very excited and proud of his accomplishment. We journeyed on. The other bus turned around and followed us ... their driver was not willing to take the risk. But we were relieved that we had finally found some larger roads, paved roads. There were still piles of tires or stumps in the road, but enough had been moved so we could get through.

We didn't anticipate any more problems, but we were wrong. Yes, the roads were passable but they had not been swept or cleaned of another item used to block a road ... nails! However, driving on bald tires is not an unusual thing for the buses, so the driver knew where to go. We stopped at one out-of-the-way station, then someone's home. After two flat tires and hours later, it was dark. People were starting to fall asleep, exhausted after all the excitement.

I have to admit that the driver's spirit was to be admired. We were now driving in darkness. There were a few lights of homes scattered in the distance. I didn't check the moon but it must have been a sliver because the night was as black as coal.

The driver asked who was getting off at Azogues. We raised our hands. However, he must have been too tired or forgotten because I was looking out the window and saw the exit for Azogues pass before my eyes. Much later, after we came into the city limits of Cuenca. I used my flashlight to read our travel book to see what was available in lodging.

After thirteen hours on the bus, we were ready for a bath and food. Lee said, "Choose anyplace, I don't care."

El Dorado Hotel/Empresa Hotelera Cuenca was an older hotel downtown by the main square. It was perfect, costing more than our cabin in Banos, but still worth it. The receptionist found it humorous that her guests arrived with backpacks and baseball hats instead of rental cars and luggage. We didn't care. It was the perfect place for us.

After we told her of our journey that day, she gave us as a gift from the hotel, tickets for two free beverages in the upstairs lounge. Before crashing for the night, we went upstairs, sat in comfortable chairs sipping our papaya juice and rum, and felt like we were now the princess and prince of Ecuador.

* * *

RISING EARLY, WE LEFT the hotel to explore the market, which we knew was nearby. We had read in our travel book about Cuenca's beautiful flower market, but this was beyond the description! It was over by a church, on the square, with the other dry good and food stalls. On our arrival, we headed toward the farthest corner of the area with the flowers. The bright morning sun and the bursting vivid blossoms were wonderful! I did sneak a few pictures of the grand displays of cut flowers; there were also a few potted ones. We were the only tourists so I felt very shy about taking photographs. After finding a place for breakfast, we returned to the hotel.

Before leaving the El Dorado again, we asked if there was any

way to go to the markets at Gualaceo and Chordeleg, known for their fruits and their jewelry. The receptionist said she'd have to investigate because Sunday was the first day of Mardi Gras and shops were shut down to celebrate.

We decided to return to the market; it was an opportunity to witness a normal shopping day for the Ecuadorians. Many women wore colored shawls; both sexes wore felt hats and some western-ized dress. But the most noticeable feature was their small stature, which may have accounted for their ability to work the beans on the steep floor of the mountains. We were relieved that the locals seemed to welcome us at the market. Saturday was our only day on the trip, so far, that everything was open. It was great to browse. Lee purchased a sweater made of llama wool and I bought some wool scarves for friends. Obviously, with knapsacks, we couldn't pick up too much. We went into a fabric store and bought a yard of cloth for an artist friend who made quilts and would love a sample of the local fabric. The sun was out and the people's spir-its were high. How could they not help but be relieved? Their political situation was resolved; El Loco (who they called "The Thief") was out of their lives and now they had doubled the reason to be festive with Mardi Gras on their agenda.

Returning to the hotel and walking through the lobby, the receptionist informed us that a taxi/guide would be by to take us tomorrow at 8 a.m. He would spend the day with us and drive us to the markets. Relieved that we didn't need to take a bus again, Lee and I were walking to our room when we noticed a television on. The patrols and military were still in Quito, and even though we knew things were settled, the images didn't look so good. The news channel was CNN. "Oh, my goodness," I said. "My sister watches CNN every minute she can. She will be panic-struck wondering where we are. We never gave them any agenda so they might think we're in Quito. I'd better call."

So I did. Sue figured that we got away from Quito but was curious about what had happened. My mother doesn't watch much TV; we hoped she had missed it. However, I was wrong, because many of mom's friends were well-traveled and one, in particular, knew we were visiting Ecuador, where she had gone. Bernice had alerted Mom to what was happening.

Going back out onto the streets for dinner, we found that Mardi Gras had started and what that meant to teenagers: water balloons. We witnessed one pickup truck carrying ten people in the back throwing balloons at everyone (including tourists). What a disaster! In the older section where we stayed, there were a lot of buildings with balconies. They too were the source of balloon throwers and anyone walking under the balcony was drenched. I was happy that some had a good enough arm to fling water balloons and hit the kids in pickups.

We made it a block down the street and ate our dinner in peace and in dry clothes, but we did not make it back without incident. Lee and I, plus a hotel clerk who was coming to work, were drenched all at once. We laughed (but not very hard) and she was livid at her wet uniform. The others greeted her with, "Remember, we did it too just a few years ago?"

The receptionist came after us as we were walking to our room. "I forgot to tell you," she said, "if you are taking any small airplanes in the next few days, the airport in Cuenca is closed for Mardi Gras."

"What a great country," I said. "First they all go on strike and close down everything to make a point to the government and now they're closing down to celebrate for Mardi Gras. They must have a long life expectancy with such a great set of values. No one appears to be starving. Everyone looks healthy and we've seen little poverty."

"I agree," Lee said, grabbing my hand. "Let's go upstairs and look out over the cityscape, have some papaya juice and philosophize about it." We stayed in the hotel that night, very happy that we had a window in an upstairs lounge where we could watch the city lights without getting wet.

* * *

WE RECEIVED A CALL from the desk bright and early. Our taxi was there, and the driver would take us to the markets. We had agreed to hire him for six hours. The cost was $30, but after our twelve hours the day before on a bus, we were ready to ride more comfortably.

The receptionist told us that the driver, José, spoke English. His vocabulary was similar to our Spanish (basic words, and not the ability to converse, just survive). We all smiled a lot, pointed and pretended we understood one another. Fortunately, we had brought our guidebook and maps so we could tell where we were going. The day was sunny and the scenery beautiful. All was well in our world. Our driver honked and passed a bus. We recognized one of the passengers from the day before. He had long hair and wore bright clothes. He was sitting on the roof with a few other locals, hanging on to the metal ridge which had been installed to restrain the luggage. It looked very precarious—uncomfortable and hot. But he didn't look at all unhappy, talking away to someone next to him.

As we drove along, we soon noticed the traffic was slowing: there had been an avalanche on the other side of the river. José said it had happened some time ago, but meanwhile, all the passengers on the buses had to get off, walk across the river on a small bridge and board another bus which would then take them the rest of the way.

The bridge was made from fallen trees, lined up and held together by some unseen force. When it was our turn, we noisily and slowly drove across. Next, we drove on a bulldozed trail wide enough for two vehicles. On some sections of the trail, we had to wait and hug the edge so the approaching vehicle could move past us down the narrow dirt path. Looking away from the river, the landslide was very obvious, the brown sandy soil had sloughed and loosely hung to the hillside, looking like gravel, piled to its highest possibility.

The autos and buses slanted one way or another as they gingerly made their way along the river bank. I wonder how the guys on the top of the bus would feel, falling one way or another like a floating rollercoaster car. How long would it take before things were back to normal—or was this normal? Conversational Spanish was my next goal. Too much information was not available with limited Spanish and few English-speaking natives.

When we arrived at Gualaceo, José stopped by a park. We

walked by his side but felt out of place in the setting since there were only Ecuadorians there. Lee bent to whisper, "You look stunning in your sunglasses. Everyone is jealous of me." I smiled and held my head high. No one seemed to mind us. It appeared to be a Sunday picnic area, people were playing games and two families were roasting whole pigs. Mardi Gras was a time to eat and party and everyone seemed to be in the spirit.

After the park, José took us to the market. It was spectacular: awnings covered some goods but other displays were placed on blankets thrown on the ground. Few had umbrellas. One small girl sat looking over the crowd, peeling some skin off the onions, making them look fresh for purchase. Little sisters in organza pink dresses were buying some taffy from a vendor. I took very few pictures and always stood behind Lee to camouflage my activity. We felt privileged to be there, but very conspicuous. We stopped for an orange soda and a cookie at a bakery on the square, treating our guide to one as well. After our snack, we all felt revived to continue.

The countryside was quiet traveling down the road to Chor-deleg. Arriving at the square, only two stores were open because of the Mardi Gras celebration. The area is known for its silver. Not being into jewelry, the mines would have interested us more but they were closed as well. Across the square, a goat stood on top of a bus, probably wondering what in the hell he was doing up there. (I assume his owner would be riding with him when the bus left unless goats have gymnastic ability.)

José took us down a few side streets to check out the shops. "Please stop," I said. "There's a gallery open."

Lee and I went inside.

"Welcome," a petite woman said. "My name is Andrea. This is

an artist's co-op and any questions you have I will try to answer."

"This artist is very talented," Lee said, as he walked over to a large ceramic plate with animalistic characters parading across the surface.

"They reflect the artifacts from the Incan ruins at Ingapirca, 80 kilometers from here. One of our artists is from the neighboring village of Canar and has grown up painting the figures. She loves painting the monkey and turtle that are part of the carvings found there," Andrea replied.

"I love her work," Lee said. "I'm an amateur sculptor in clay and get my inspiration from Mayans and Pacific Northwest Coast Indians of North America, but have not seen these Incan figures. I wish we could buy this large plate but we'll have to get a small one because we are backpackers and cannot possibly get a large one back safely."

"I understand," Andrea said.

When we made the purchase, she gave us a small woven basket as a gift. We said our goodbyes and left with our memento.

It was a wonderful day driving and absorbing the sights of the countryside … what a luxury to have our own wheels!

Retracing our steps, the ride home was as interesting as earlier that day except the avalanche area was even busier; several people were walking by and trying to sell their wares. Newspapers, crystallized sugar candy and pieces of melon were available in little plastic bags. The melon looked delicious. The candy looked like sweet marzipan. Peering in our window they stopped to ask if we were interested. José spoke with them and purchased some peanuts.

We stopped before the bridge, watching all the riders scrambling off the bus and over the river to switch buses. We waited as the bus turned around, see-sawing back and forth endless times before the driver made the 360-degree turn. Two men were yelling directions as the driver turned, little by little. I cannot imagine how they could manage in the dark or if they were having a bad day.

Finally, it was our turn, and over we went. People walked around us like fish swimming around a rock in a stream. This time they were coming from another bus and eager to catch the one that had just turned around. It was a real struggle for those who were older or had large, heavy packages. Because of their handicaps, they would get the worst seats (although I'm sure some of the elderly were taken care of).

Lee mentioned that the water balloon activity was nonexistent in the country and that it must have been a city-dweller activity. Watching carefully as we walked into the hotel, we avoided a group driving by, feeling like we were getting the hang of it.

For supper that evening we were told of a new restaurant around the corner. After walking through a door, we came into a courtyard that had tables on the lawn and awnings hanging from the neighboring walls to protect us from sun or rain. At one end stood a cooking house and an adjoining enclosed dining area, obviously, for the rainy season. It was the first week open for the new restaurant. The owner had left Cuenca and moved to Puerto Rico, returning as a bilingual (Spanish and English) citizen with the desire to open a restaurant. He told us that he opened even during the strike to practice getting the food ready. "No one reprimanded us, but thought it was a good idea," he said.

Since the entire city, except us, knew that he was closing early for the holiday, we were the last to be seated. Asking the chef's recommendation, Lee and I both ordered shrimp in coconut sauce which was delicious. Before leaving, we sipped a delicious cup of black coffee as we watched and listened to the sounds of them putting the restaurant to bed.

The owners' small child came running over to smile and put her fist in her mouth in greeting. Her mother shortly followed and told us in English she was Puerto Rican adding, "I believe I will love Cuenca."

After our wonderful *repas*, we raced around the corner, avoiding a water balloon by inches. Lee and I came laughing into the hotel and told the receptionist about the wonderful restaurant and meal. As we were talking she said something to a man standing in the lobby.

Breathless, he returned after running around the corner to check to see if the restaurant was still open. A lady told him it was closed for the evening.

"I'm sorry," I said. "You didn't stay around long enough to hear me say we were the last customers." We all laughed together.

CHAPTER FOUR

Riobamba and back

Before we left the next morning, we thanked the concierge and headed to the bus station. Lee and I had decided to go as far as Riobamba and stay the night. That would put us halfway to Quito, plus we would see another city.

Most of the roads had been cleared by then although the burned tires still lay in the ditches, lending clutter to an otherwise clean-looking roadside. The ride was quiet and uneventful. Mardi Gras week occupied the citizens with partying and parades and festivals. From the concierge in Cuenca we had learned (confirming our suspicions) that water balloons would be part of Riobamba. "It's a tradition in larger cities. Beware," she said.

She also advised us to explore the parks and the city square to see if there were a few stalls open. "With a holiday and Monday, not many vendors will be around. Oh," she added, "notice the different styles of hats. You'll see more white ones; the style and color change with the area."

* * *

WE FELT LUCKY TO find a perfect small hotel called Hotel el Cisne for $12 when we arrived in Riobamba. Our room was on the second floor, with a window facing the street where we could look down at all the action.

Dropping our gear on the bed (except for my umbrella), we went out for a long walk. It was very quiet, with only a few places open, but we needed some exercise. Using my umbrella to shield us, we avoided getting wet; sometimes, it felt like we were fencing with the balloon-throwers.

"Too bad we didn't get the name of the place where Rita was staying here," I said to Lee.

"What are you talking about?" Lee asked.

"You know, the gal we shared the cab with after we landed and dropped at Moby the Grape? Wasn't this where she was coming to teach English?"

He laughed and squeezed my shoulder. "You're somethin' else. Come on. Let's explore."

That evening, we found an Asian restaurant. A very cute waitress worked there; at least that's what the water balloon throwers felt. They kept pitching the balloons in through the open double paneled glass doorway.

The waitress kept smiling until one of the throwers with a heavy arm broke a panel in the door with the loaded balloon. The owner, already furious with the wet floor, ran shaking his fist out into the street ... such is the price of a pretty waitress during Mardi Gras! After dinner, we went back to our hotel and observed the activity below through our window. I searched our travel book for the info on the variety of hats that we'd seen. It was not a surprise to discover each area had a style, color and material (most used felt) of its own. But what was fascinating was the information on the Panama hat. It was made in Ecuador and exported to Panama. No one knows how they got the credit for the name. Interestingly, few Ecuadorians wore Panama hats.

As I was telling the information to Lee, he unwrapped our purchase from the day before and sat admiring it. "When we get back, I said, "I'll be curious to see how these figures are reflected in your sculptures. I love the masks you've done that we have on our wall. Especially, the one you did for me of the spitting dog."

"You're just biased," Lee said.

"I know I am, but you're good, and you've sold several pieces at our gallery and they didn't know you from a hole in the ground."

He laughed. "Nicely put."

* * *

RETURNING TO QUITO THE next day, Lee and I walked into the Hotel Amaranta. It was like coming back home. Danielle was at the desk and greeted us with a smile. "Well if it isn't my American travelers. I figured that when you didn't come back you made the bus out of Quito."

There was no activity in the lobby so she asked all about the trip. She listened, and at times interrupted to ask questions. After a few minutes, Danielle said, "I am very glad you are safe. Please tell your friends and countrymen that my people are peaceful and fun-loving and how they united to get rid of El Loco."

* * *

THE NEXT DAY WE tried, once again, to phone the farmers that our Peace Corps friends said to contact. This time they answered and were aghast that we had come in such a turbulent time, and amused at our decision to go to Banos.

Lee and I spent a day in Quito browsing local markets and stores. We were on a scavenger hunt of sorts, seeking out a mask or small sculpture as a reminder of our trip and also a present for a bibliophile-friend who wanted a publication from Ecuador. We found him a book at Libri Mundi, Quito's most comprehensive book store. For ourselves, we purchased a papier-mâché tiger's head mask that we found at the market. It was beautiful. I stowed it under the seat in front of me on the plane ride home and hoped the mask would not be destroyed (last year, I gave it to a friend who runs a Montessori school). Before we left, we tucked in a visit to the museum. Looking at sculpture was an interest of ours; Lee because he was a sculptor and I favored the more primitive or folk artists even for our gallery.

We stopped back at Café Cultura to thank Mateo for the suggestions and assistance he had given us. Sadly, he was off that night. We left him a note and then had some soup and bread as our evening meal.

Our last evening on the rooftop was calm and peaceful. Quito looked beautiful, nestled in the valley as it had at the beginning of our visit. The pollution in the air might still exist, but the political pollution had cleared.

Lee and I toasted one another, "To us, and the resilience of our fellowmen."

Acknowledgments

The process of publishing is like directing an orchestra and working with the musicians until the piece is ready. I thank Beth Bracale for her never-ending ear and feedback, Peg Asensio for her rendering of the passports, Michael Anne Johnson for fine-tuning my photos and Wendy Walton Mishne for her enthusiasm. Of course, my nieces and nephews Valerie, Meredith, Britta, Dave, Sara and Christopher were constantly involved with surveys on the cover, etc. and I cherish their input.

Northeast Ohio Writers group heard and critiqued the journals when we were regularly meeting pre-Covid-19. The Kingsville Public Library was absolutely stellar, giving me endless technical help (especially Brandon and his work on the cover). Christine Pride, a publishing veteran, read the manuscript and gave me some valuable suggestions. Laura DeMarco did the copy editing and author MaryAnn Myers gave it a final read for good luck. Formatting was done by The Book Cover Whisperer: OpenBookDesign.biz.

It was my great fortune to have such a wonderful team. Thank you all.

About the Author

JUDI'S FAMILY LEGACY IS WRITING. After graduating from the University of Iowa, she began her career co-authoring fourteen scientific publications. Years into her profession, Judi shifted gears and went into the creative arena. She established Pentagon Gallery and Frame, Inc. in Cleveland, Ohio, representing area artists for 25 years until the death of her partner-in-life, Leland Emerson. For years she has journaled and written numerous pieces of prose, poetry and stories. Born a Franklin and following in the path of two of her Swedish grandparents who wrote their memoirs, Judi penned her autobiography reveling in the magic of her small town's Scandinavian environment. *Letters to the Chief: A Minnesota Childhood* was published in 2020 by Wisdom Editions (A Calumet imprint) and has won three awards. Her new book, *A Glimpse of the Other Americas: A Backpacker's Memoir,* was released in 2022.

Judi spends her creative writing hours sequestered in her house on the Lake Erie shoreline. Today she travels between her homes in Cleveland and North Kingsville On-the-Lake. She continues to write, work as a medical advocate, and visit with family and friends. There are at least two other books to come. A break from family tradition, these are children's stories titled *Judi's Tales and Fables Volume I and II.* Please follow the author on www.judilifton.com.